G+DW

Seein

Seeing Straight

Winning over dyslexia

Dot Croall

Edited by Pat Wraight

Marshall Pickering

Marshall Morgan and Scott
Marshall Pickering
3 Beggarwood Lane, Basingstoke,
Hants RG23 7LP, UK

First published in 1986 by Marshall Morgan and Scott Publications Ltd
Part of the Marshall Pickering Holdings Group
A subsidiary of the Zondervan Corporation

British Library CIP Data

Croall, Dot
Seeing straight: winning over dyslexia.
1. Dyslexic children — Biography
I. Title II. Wright, Pat
362.1'98928553'00924 RC394.W6

ISBN 0-551-01350-8

Text set in Times by Input Typesetting Ltd, London
Printed in Great Britain by Anchor Brendon Ltd, Tiptree, Essex

Contents

Acknowledgement

I would like to thank the many people who have been involved in the life of my family and those who have spent time and energy helping me put this real life story into print.

I want to particularly thank Andy, my husband, and Paul, Barry and Ruth for allowing some of the very personal areas of their lives to be exposed to public examination in the hope that parents and children will be helped to look at their own lives and relationships in a positive way.

Above all I thank our Father God who has brought about this lovely miracle in our lives and strengthened us to face adverse circumstances.

Dot Croall

Foreword by Roy Castle

It is now more than four years since Paul was healed of his learning difficulties. In the time that has passed, the handicap problems which had once frustrated him have been replaced by much joy: in his achievements at college and in attaining a degree place on a Computer Science Course at Wolverhampton Polytechnic, and above all in his communication which has helped him to forge new relationships.

But this is only part of Paul's story. For the themes of this book are complex and all-embracing. In fact the themes are not focused on Paul alone, rather they encompass a family's growth and development.

Although it can be said that I contribute to the story in some way, my great pleasure is in writing this foreword so that the experiences the Croall family faced together — their laughter, sorrow, hopes and fears — can be of help to others. And yet the Croalls' story is also a living testimony which bears witness to their Christian values. They persevered and trusted in the knowledge that all would come right for Paul in the end.

Seeing Straight illustrates in a number of ways the steps Dot and Andy Croall took to observe, determine and treat Paul's learning difficulties in their own way. The methods they adopted, their experiences and solutions are an example for all readers who encounter learning difficulties, in themselves or in those close to them. This book is a pictorial of God moving and working in the lives of an ordinary family and in a community as a whole.

Roy Castle
March 1986

1

The Best Laid Plans . . .

IT WAS WITH GREAT JOY and anticipation that our first son was born on a lovely spring day in April 1967. We had been the ideal prospective parents, having read all the latest information about childbirth and rearing, the best diets, the most up-to-date knowledge of child growth and development. Andy, my husband, was on a social work course and being taught how to care for baby's needs before and after birth, by a renowned paediatrician. I was secretary at our local doctor's surgery, and my ante and post-natal care was the best!

But how we came to be living in Beaconsfield, Buckinghamshire, instead of our native Liverpool is a story in itself.

Back in 1963, I had just completed a two year course at the Bible Training Institute in Glasgow. I felt to succeed in college was to go abroad as a missionary and the pressure was on to apply to missionary societies. But somehow I knew this wasn't for me. But what should I do? If I went back home I would be thought of as a failure and my two years at college wasted. Yet deep within my heart I knew I was to go back to Liverpool.

The end of term came and I dreaded the last day. The fear of what others would think gripped me. Then, quite clearly, I realised I didn't have to perform in a certain way to be accepted by God. I was accepted and loved by him whether I was in Africa, India, or

Liverpool. Somehow that week God showed himself to me in a new way: I became so aware of his love and his acceptance, and I knew without a doubt that he had a plan for my life, a unique plan. A plan which, had I known what it was to involve for all our family, I would not have chosen to follow.

It was October, autumn had arrived and the trees were changing colour with the leaves falling gently to the ground. And to me it was like autumn in my life; everything seemed to be falling from me. I had lost my status as a student, I felt my friends had stopped thinking about me and praying for me. I was twenty-three years old, and my college friends were all marrying or going abroad somewhere. I felt sure that one day I would marry but it seemed so remote at that time. But, back to Liverpool I went and, of course, almost immediately the doubts began. Had I made the right decision? Should I have gone to Africa or India? . . . My mind was whirling with these thoughts when into my life walked Andy, the proverbial tall, dark stranger.

Although we lived only a mile apart and had attended the same school – even being in the same class as Juniors – we had never known each other as children. Following Grammar School, Andy had gone on to Liverpool University to study electrical engineering and I had gone to Bible College. After three years of a four year course, however, Andy's university career came to a sudden end. Somehow his studies had taken second place to other activities in which he got involved. Quite apart from being elected President of the Engineering Society, Andy ran a youth club, became involved in CND marches and, on one occasion, demonstrated outside the American Embassy disguised as Fidel Castro! One day it was suggested that perhaps it would be better if he left the university and found another way of fulfilling his interests.

The next step was to take up a three year traineeship with D. Napier & Son (English Electric Co. Ltd.), but during his second year of training Andy knew that there was another pressure on his life and he sensed that God was wanting to change his direction yet again. He had this overwhelming conviction that he should be involved with people, especially those with broken hearts resulting in mental illness. This was to be a massive step. What was he to tell his employers? His parents? His friends? But he faced the questions and the accusations – 'Fancy throwing away a good education!': 'You have security in your job': 'All the money it has cost to keep you at college': 'You will have to re-train': 'Fancy dealing with people's problems all day' – and many more.

Soon after this he was offered another post with the English Electric Company at their Netherton branch as Assistant to the Personnel Manager. This was a change from electrical engineering but he accepted the job while he contemplated the future of his traineeship. Then, one morning, his boss threw a newspaper on his desk and said 'You should apply for this, Andy'. It was for a post as Mental Welfare Officer in High Wycombe, Buckinghamshire.

Meanwhile, the church we attended in Liverpool was holding a children's mission and part of the preparation was that the helpers should meet early in the morning to pray. As Andy and I lived quite near to each other we began to walk home together at 7.30 am on the dark November mornings. Gradually romance blossomed and I realised how serious he was when, one snowy morning, he came to our house and buried me in the snow in the garden!

We attended the Peoples' Church in Liverpool at that time and one day a dear older man spoke to Andy saying, 'God has annointed you to bring healing and deliverance to many'. It was so out of character for this man to do such a thing that it confirmed to Andy that he should be applying for the new position as a Mental Welfare Officer. So he applied, not knowing or fully understanding what the job entailed.

It was September 1964, when Andy left Liverpool and moved south and I joined him the following spring. Everything looked so clean and green in this lovely county of Buckinghamshire. Moving from my home near the Liverpool football ground to an area of such wealth and materialism was quite a cultural shock. And yet we still found loneliness, frustration, and unhappiness. We were yet to meet the many people whom God had waiting for us.

The search began for accommodation and it was very difficult. We had no money for a deposit on a house, and the price of flats or bed-sits was extortionate, if you could fine one, that was. Another problem we had was that we did not know the area in which to settle. During the six months Andy had been in lodgings he had looked around the whole of south Bucks, visiting towns, estate agents, football clubs and churches.

The churches appeared to be almost lifeless, and the ministers so weary. We wished we could pick somewhere else, but no, we were pretty sure by then that our area had to be Beaconsfield. Surely we must be crazy! It was a lovely town, but so expensive! The area where film and T.V. stars lived. The whole idea seemed impossible but somehow we felt this was the town God wanted us in. What a conflict – did we trust that God was with us? Was he really leading us to this town?

In my final months in Liverpool I had been working for an Orthodontic Surgeon in Carnegie Clinic, Oxford Street. He was a very nice man, very professional with pinstripes and all! He arranged for us to visit a friend of his in Chalfont St. Giles, near Beaconsfield, and he and his wife invited us over for lunch. We duly arrived at the driveway to this beautiful home in our little Standard 8 car which seemed so small as we drove up to the house! But once inside we relaxed. It was so lovely to meet wealthy people who loved Jesus. The gentleman was so gracious, wisdom poured from his lips. We had a beautiful meal with all the best trimmings, served on silver dishes – a little different to fish and chips in the paper! Then, as we prepared to leave, our host said to us, 'I think you should be in Beaconsfield'. What a shock! So we looked at flats and bedsits, never even contemplated a house – we just couldn't afford one. It was so frustrating, everything was financially miles out of our reach, but now we knew that this was the area we had to be in.

By this time Andy was a Trainee Mental Welfare Officer/Social Worker employed on a very low salary. We had calculated that £250 pa was all we could possibly afford for accommodation. In fact we discovered that young couples generally moved out of Beaconsfield to set up home! Have you ever cried to God in a situation where there appears to be no answer? We did. We said, 'God, if you want us here you will have to find us somewhere to live' – at under £250 per year!

One Sunday morning we visited the Baptist Church in Beaconsfield and a lady approached us to ask if we would like to come over for supper that evening. We were glad to accept but, naïve about southern customs, we had our evening meal and went over for supper. To us supper was a piece of toast and jam, possibly a piece of cheese, but certainly not a three course meal! Arriving at the home of John and Anne Carey we smelt this lovely aroma wafting out into the hallway. We had boobed! We glanced at each other and decided it was better not to admit having already eaten, so said nothing and managed to eat another meal!

As we chatted to John and Anna, we discovered that John was a General Practitioner in the town. Suddenly he asked, 'Where are you going to live when you marry?' We didn't know, and both looked blank, but without waiting for an answer John said, 'I would like you to have our flat'. What flat? Where? How many rooms? How much? It's still five months before we marry and we will not be able to afford it before then, if we can afford it then. We knew that to rent a bedsit, if you could get one, was at least £6 per week. Then we discovered this flat had three bedrooms, lounge, kitchen and bathroom, and its own private entrance. Surely we could never do it. It sounded really nice, right in the heart of the Old Town, Beaconsfield. The flat was in a property which was two hundred years old but was being newly renovated. John said he would talk to his two partners the next day and work out a price. By the time the senior partner telephoned us on the Monday, we had really dismissed the idea because we thought it was sure to be £15 per week. The other problem was timing. The house was being renovated to make this beautiful old building into three surgeries and a self-contained flat. We knew only too well that such a major renovation could take months. So, by the time the phone rang, we were not at all hopeful. However, as Dr. Michael Watkins spoke to Andy, my heart leapt. I could see by the look on his face that he was hearing good news. It was, the price was to be £250 per year! What's more, the flat was completed two weeks before our wedding day! We sat down together and wept at this miracle, little knowing this was just the start of many, many more miracles in our lives.

It was into this situation that our son, Paul, was born. We really planned for this baby, we wanted him so much. I remember the joy when I first felt him move within my womb . . . it was amazing. As we crossed the days off the calendar we became more and more excited. We read all the books we could find about pregnancy and babies, and prepared his bedroom in yellow – just in case it was a girl! Finally, two weeks late, he decided to arrive, and was born on Monday afternoon at 1.45 pm. As Andy held him he prayed and thanked God for this little person, and so the first name Paul ever heard was Jesus!

The total responsibility of having a child really struck me when Paul was born. It struck me again when our second son, Barry, was born, and again two years later when Ruth completed our family. I was overcome with the realisation that how these little bundles of life saw the world was going to be through my eyes. It was not so much what I had to say, but I knew they would pick up my attitudes to life, to men, society, home, nature, school and many others things. Experience had taught me that the first five years in a child's life are so important and that it is during these years that a child's character is formed. He learns to sit up, crawl, walk, speak, touch, handle, these things and many others are built into his character. For a toddler, a heap of mud is heaven! And to pour water along the hallway and watch it form streams brings much joy to a child, though not so much to the parents! But a wide variety of experiences are a necessary part of any child's learning process. We parents have all experienced times when a child is so involved in play that he or she is oblivious to his or her surroundings. It is so easy to feel it is a time of nappies, washing, crying, and hard work. How we need to realise these years are so important to each child, and not be so busy that we miss them! It is a time of putting into the child our view of life, our view of the world and of standards that matter to us.

We settled in our flat with joy, excitement and anticipation and began to reach out to the community round about seeking to find the purpose of God in bringing us to Beaconsfield. We did not have to wait very long. Right from the beginning for some reason Andy and I attracted people who had difficulties. This just seemed to happen but we know, deep down within us, that God – this Being we sometimes don't understand – wanted to reveal himself in all his love to hurting people. People who are homeless, or have suffered the trauma of divorce, or bereavement, misunderstanding or rejection. And not only to reveal Himself but to heal their hurts and broken hearts and to give them a new model of a Father who really loves them. He wasn't going to give up on them. He was for them and not against them. So many of us get an image of God from our early childhood as a man with a big long beard who is out to make us miserable and condemn us.

These days the world is full of hurting people. Those who as a child or an adult have gone through the pain of a divorce; a father leaving home; a mother who just couldn't cope anymore. Children who are torn between one parent and the other. Children who feel they can never live up to what their parents expect of them. They feel everything they do is criticised – the way they dress, how they stay out late, their friends, their school work. Sometimes they just long to be accepted not for what they do but for who they are.

One thing we decided when we planned to have children was that we would always be honest with them, even if it caused traumas. I am not saying you should over-expose your child to too many facts all at once, but what I am saying is that in the practical details of life there is a need for honesty. For example – you might say 'Johnny, if you touch that again I will smack you'. So Johnny touches it again and you shout at him. Very early on he learns that what you say you don't mean. I am not advocating smacking a child, it is just an example. Another may be – 'You won't get your pudding if you don't eat your main meal'. Then with a half-eaten meal you hand over the pudding. I am not saying you should stop your child having pudding, but that you should not threaten what you don't intend to do. It might help to give the child a much smaller helping of what you know he will eat. We feel somehow we have to win a war over food. Relax in it. When 'Ruthie' was tiny I got very worried because she would hardly eat anything that I felt was a 'good proper meal'. But she would eat as much fruit as she could get, and bread and jam. One day I experienced, as an onlooker, a most disturbing scene. I was in a cafe and near me was a mother with a two or three year old boy. This mother was practically pushing a cheese sandwich into his mouth, amidst protests that he wanted crisps like his little friends. The bitterness in his eyes, the sadness in his cries, and the total frustration of this mum who was out to win this battle really distressed me and showed me we should not treat mealtimes as battle grounds. Children don't need as much as we think they do. It is better to win your child than the battle over food. I relaxed and joined Ruth, who in her teens will eat anything.

The most well-meaning parents say some awful things to their children without realising the devastating effect this has on their lives. It is not because we don't love our children, but we repeat what has been said to us when we were children. Occasionally we realise how things have hurt us and correct our attitudes before they escape our lips.

I know from experience the damage that can be caused through something that was said without thought to me when I was young. I know my mum will understand if I share what happened to help other parents with their children.

My mum and dad were the most loving parents. Nothing was too much trouble. My dad died a few years ago but my mum is still very much alive and living in Liverpool. She is a lovely lady and has always opened her home to anyone who wished to come in. I can remember tramps coming to our door and she would never turn them away. She would not give them money but would always give them food and drink. Each Sunday she provided tea for thirty to forty young people at our home and during the Teddy Boy era, our house used to be full of these boys from off the streets playing billiards and table tennis. She never seemed to tire of them. Down the years I think she has entertained many angels and perhaps has been an angel to many as well.

My mum came from a big, Catholic family, but my dad had seen the bitter side of life. He was brought up in the Fazakerley Cottage Homes because his father had left home and his mother couldn't afford to keep the children. When fourteen years old he came out, but during his first few months of freedom he had a motor accident and was in hospital for a year. This would be about 1925. The years of Depression followed, and he became very disillusioned with life and declared himself to be an atheist. So from this background my parents married. Times were hard, money was short, there was no prospect of work. My dad said that when they first married he would go to the fish shop and buy a 'cod's head for the cat' which they would eat for a family meal.

Then the Second World War threatened. I was born a month before war broke out. We lived in a council house, and bombs dropped all around us. I was the third baby in the family, and they were very hard times. You can imagine the pressure my mum and dad were under.

Something that was said to me at this time really hurt me, although I was under five years old. I know now that it wasn't meant, but in my formative years it was built into my being or personality as 'truth'. It has been shown that from birth to five years we have, as it were, tape recordings being made inside us when we hear things and believe them to be the truth. Have you ever heard yourself say something and thought, 'Oh, dear, where did that come from?' For example – 'If you are a naughty girl the policeman will get you', 'If you do that I won't love you any more', 'Be quiet, children should be seen and not heard', 'Stop asking questions', 'Why can't you be like Mary Jones down the street', 'People won't like you if you do that', 'You'll be a nuisance, they won't want you'. There are many more things that slip out of our mouths without us realising the harm they can do. These are the things which become formed in our beings, and which we believe are truth. On occasions these tapes switch on without us really thinking about them. Happily there is good news, you don't have to go on living with these attitudes or hang-ups for ever. But in my own experience things said in childhood affected me until well into my married life. For years and years I felt I was not acceptable. To me, to be acceptable was to do everything right, to be perfect, have a nice figure, never a hair out of place, tastefully chosen clothes, lovely clean house, nice clean sheets. I always felt I should be like someone else, but not me! My schooling had been a bad experience. Being caned at six years of age for simply jumping in someone else's rope reinforced in me my earlier learning that to be accepted I had to be perfect. So I felt it was best to put a nice smile on my face and just be good. I thought I was totally stupid, I was not like the others, so although I went to school I emotionally opted out. The pressure of having to perform in a certain way, and write in a certain manner (e.g. making my writing lean forwards, when my natural inclination was to write straight upwards) was agony because I believed I was stupid, my standard was not the highest, so to me it was no good. In a nutshell, I felt to be loved I had to be perfect. Sometimes I would look around other people and think 'I can't be as stupid as all that'. I never had any difficulty getting boy-friends when some of my friends never got asked out. When I met Andy I was staggered that he thought I knew more about some things than he did, when he had been to University! Sadly, I had set standards for myself that there was no hope of attaining and at times this led me into real depression. Remember for me to be loved I had to be perfect.

These hurts deep within me showed up very little as we set up home in our lovely flat. But as more and more young people came for help the pressure began to increase. They needed more than a casual chat, they needed real time-consuming help and security. So we took them in to live with us. It was an unusual home which could best be described as an extended family. Our own family unit consisted of Andy, my husband, Paul eighteen months, myself and Barry on the way. We also cared for a number of teens and twenties who had been in the care of the Social Services, or who had been victims of divorced or separated families. On the whole they were homeless young people, some from very affluent respectable homes but experiencing much heartache, never being able to live up to the standards that had been set for them. We also had people helping us in the care of these young folk. It was a very demanding task but we had such a love for these kids who had seen heartache and pain and we felt we had an answer to their deep insecurity. We laughed, cried, wept and shouted over them and for them. How do you show a teenager who has been rejected by her mother, then rejected by her step-mother, that God loves her? We found it was by being Christ to her, not preaching at her but practising love, whatever the cost. Sometimes we would only have four people, at others we had to rent some bedrooms in the house next door when there were eighteen people in 'the family'. It was a very rewarding four years, although it took much time and energy. There were times when I was so tired, so worn out, struggling with my toddlers, not enough money and sometimes not enough time. I felt as if I was on a treadmill – just performing the necessary tasks, taking time to be with and care for the children, and also spending time with Andy, my husband. It was a hard task to bring all these demands on my life into some kind of order.

So being a wife, mother, housemother of eight plus at times, and counsellor, my task was impossible. My standard was such that I had to be a perfect wife, lover, hostess, housekeeper, mother, to always have nice hair and matching clothes. Anything less than this and I felt Andy would not love me any more. You can imagine the aggravation this caused. I would blame Andy for my high standards because I felt he was expecting perfection from me. Things would run smoothly for a while but then I would blow up. Another thing that showed its ugly head now and again was that, for some reason, I felt I was going to be replaced. Don't get me wrong, I didn't think Andy was going to be unfaithful to me and there was always someone willing to help if I was pregnant, which happened every two years until our family was complete. Poor Andy, I would allow my suspicions to make me really upset with him. I thank God that he gave me an understanding man who was gently able to show me that my fears were groundless. As you can imagine, I was often so angry. It was through these years of real desperation and heartache that release came for me and the family. Eventually I came to the end of my tether because Paul was late in developing. He was very late sitting up. He didn't crawl until well over twelve months old, and then backwards! My friend's baby was walking, Paul wasn't even saying 'Mama and Dada'. Already I was aware that something was wrong, but I didn't know what. I knew babies developed at different stages. We had always talked to Paul, cuddled him and I breast-fed him. This all added up to my feeling that I was stupid – and now my baby was going to be the same. This is what was going through my mind, but I could not explain it to anybody, it hurt so much.

2

The Formative Years

WHEN PAUL was about eighteen months old, he awoke from a peaceful sleep. But when I lifted him out of his cot I noticed that his left eye had turned right in. I thought at first that it was my imagination. He had lovely blue eyes, and there had never been any difficulty before. I looked again and it was like a bad dream, it was so hard to believe. I dressed him and took him downstairs. By the time we reached the kitchen his eye was normal again. When Andy arrived home I explained what had happened but by then I was beginning to wonder if it could have been my imagination. But the next day it happened again and it gradually occurred more and more frequently. On waking, or as Paul got tired, his left eye would turn right in.

I wept and wept over this. My child was not perfect. I loved him so much. Our doctor, Dr. Eileen Watkins, was very helpful and most reassuring. She made an appointment at the local hospital with Mr. Moss, the Eye Consultant. So began many weekly visits to the hospital to see the Orthoptist. Paul was so young and had only just started walking. He had to look through a binocular-type object and try to put soldiers into little boxes. And from then on he had to wear a big patch on his eye. But although he was so young he accepted it. We spent time explaining to him as simply as possible what was happening. We found he accepted his patch more easily if his Teddy wore one as well!

We have often wondered if it was the eye exercises at this very tender age that marred his development. We will never know, it is a mystery, but even before this eye problem episode, I was aware of his late development:

Sitting up at nine months
Crawling at eleven months (then backwards)
Walking at eighteen months
Speech: 'Mama' and 'Dadda' eighteen months
Additional four or five words at twenty two months, only clear speech at three years
And then difficult to strangers up to five years plus.

It still upsets me as I remember the frustration he experienced. He could not hold even large crayons to draw with. He had big problems with the manipulation of objects. Even large floor jigsaws would cause so much frustration that they would be flung across the room.

Paul's squint of twenty degrees was first noted in February 1969. The first visit to the consultant was quite traumatic for me because I was full of questions. Was it my fault? Had I done something wrong? I was seven months pregnant at the time carrying Barry and I was very large, as he was 9lbs 10ozs at birth. It was quite difficult to keep a nearly two-year-old happy in a hospital waiting room, the three quarters of an hour wait seemed like an eternity! Eventually a very nice nurse appeared and called 'Paul Croall, please'. We walked into the surgery which was so white and sterile-looking with all those big machines. The consultant, Mr. Moss, was very nice to Paul, he explained to him the procedure. He would have to have drops in his eyes for the examination and then look at pictures through the machines. Paul was quite excited and cooperated extremely well.

Mr. Moss said that Paul's squint was minimal at the moment but he would review him in three months, and in the meantime he would have to have drops inserted daily with patches on his eyes intermittently. May 1969 arrived, I had given birth to Barry in April. He was late in arriving but was a gorgeous baby, with quite a lot of hair and big brown eyes.

When we visited Mr. Moss again he said that Paul now had a constant left squint of fifteen per cent and his eye would need to be operated on. My heart sank when he explained the operation to me. Then he said that Paul would probably not be able to see for a couple of days after the operation, and you can imagine the thoughts that crossed my mind. Would he be blind? They might make a mistake. The anaesthetic might affect him. He was so young. It was only recently, when I spoke with Dr. Eileen that I realised the seriousness of the decision to operate. They felt that if the operation had been delayed Paul might have lost the sight in that eye.

November 1969 we visited the hospital again for an appointment prior to the operation. Paul explained that when he looked at things they were moving. At this stage he developed twitching eyes, but whether this was a nervous twitch, or whether he was trying to stop things moving, we do not know.

December 1969 with Paul approaching three years, and Barry eight months old, we were faced with hospitalisation. How would we cope? Paul would need me so much at this traumatic time, and Barry was just at the age when separation from his mother could be disastrous. Both Andy and I were determined that we would only give our consent for this operation if I could be allowed to stay in hospital with Paul. We had counselled many people who had suffered emotional scars from being hospitalized without somebody they loved being present with them. Research carried out on the child/parent relationships in a hospital situation showed that in the past it was felt that the child would settle better without the parent, but in fact,what happened was that the child withdrew and became institutionalised. This helped the organisation of a busy hospital routine, but in fact the child felt desolate and heartbroken.

The operation was performed at Stoke Mandeville Hospital, a hospital that is known all over the world for its lead in the medical field. We wrote to the Administrator and the Consultant, telling them we felt it to be vitally important for me to be allowed to stay in hospital with Paul. Their reply was positive. They agreed in principle, although they explained that at times this was not possible because of the shortage of beds. They now have accommodation for parents where they can sleep and be called if the child wakes in the night, which means they can be on the ward all day with the child. However, I was very fortunate to be given a bed right next to Paul's cot. We loved, cuddled, laughed, played and cried together. It was the longest ten days of my life but I would not have missed being with Paul for anything.

Paul co-operated very well. Even when it was necessary to insert drops in his eyes that would sting, he would lie flat on the floor and tell us when he was ready. Andy had spent time reasoning so much with this little chap, he could get him to do anything. It was not an authoritarian-type attitude saying 'You will if I say so' but a gentle persuasion, a loving, chiding saying, 'Come on son, it may hurt but it has to be done'. We have learned that God treats us like that, too. He doesn't get out the big stick to whack us, but gently gets alongside us and reassures us that He is out for our good. He wants the very best for us, although at times it hurts.

My mum came down from Liverpool to help Andy with Barry and the extended family and I really appreciated that because Andy was then able to bring Barry to the hospital every afternoon, where he would stay for a couple of hours. I would cuddle him, feed him, walk with him and play with him while Andy spent time with Paul.

We had really taken time to build into Paul confidence in us, and explained to him what would happen. Even as he was wheeled into the theatre on the trolley, he was so peaceful. However, one afternoon after the operation, Andy and Barry had come to visit and Paul was asleep in his cot. We sat in the Day Room talking to each other and playing with Barry. Suddenly we heard a piercing scream from Paul and wondered what on earth had happened. We rushed to his cot, where two nurses were standing. They had not wanted to disturb us in the Day Room when it was time for Paul's drops. He had been so co-operative previously when we had explained what would happen. But this time, one of the nurses had held him by force while the other one inserted the drops into his eyes. He awoke absolutely petrified. Andy was very angry with the nursing staff and he let them know it. It took a lot of time to reassure Paul after this episode. We later talked to the staff on the ward, and found they really thought this was the best way to handle toddlers. But we have found it much better to take time to talk and explain things to little ones and not to treat them as objects who have to do exactly as you say. One day they will be big enough, and stronger than you, so they won't have to obey you. If you gain their love and respect at an early age, you will find that the teenage years are so enjoyable and that there isn't always a fight to win. They will love and respect you and trust your word and will want to please you.

Paul's operation was arranged for 1 o'clock in the afternoon, which meant he could not eat or drink at all that morning. Fortunately, he was given his Pre-Med before lunch, so when the food trolley arrived he was quite sleepy. I stayed close by his side right up until he reached the Operating Theatre door. Feelings of not being able to help at all at this moment overwhelmed me. I just had to entrust him to God and this expert medical team. The Sister told me that Paul would be in the Theatre and Recovery room for about one and a half hours, which seemed an awful long time. The Sister in charge encouraged me to walk along to the canteen and have a cup of coffee. As I walked down the long corridors I wanted to shout to everybody about Paul, but they were so busy, so concerned with their own difficulties – but deep within me I sensed the presence of God. It is hard to explain, but He was assuring me that He was with me. A tremendous peace came over me and, as tears streamed down my face, I knew that God was holding on to Paul. As I approached the canteen, the looks on the faces of the majority of the people were so sad and empty. I wanted to shout out 'God can meet you in your desperate circumstances. It doesn't have to be the end.'

Exactly one and a half hours later Paul was back in his cot, unconscious, and with big bandages round his head. He looked a pathetic little soul! Fortunately he was only semi-conscious for the next two days until they removed the bandages. When they did he was very swollen and bruised and couldn't focus properly for another couple of days. Lying at his side was his big yellow duck with a bandage on its head!

Paul recovered very well from this operation, it was 100 per cent successful. We shall never know if this was part of the root of the learning/language difficulty that later became so evident. Perhaps it could play some part.

Life was hectic as usual with two little ones and a house full of young people to look after. Christmas passed and was delightful, especially as we had Paul's operation behind us. Paul and Barry were growing so fast, it was a great privilege to have been given these two little boys to care for.

September 1970 Paul started Playgroup; he was still not talking properly. It was noticeable that the other children and the staff had difficulty understanding him. He had already been to a Speech Therapist but had rejected her efforts to help. We felt it best to leave these visits for the time being and not to draw attention to his lisp. I was getting desperate. He was three years old and still he could hardly talk. He would get so frustrated with balls, big shape blocks, large jig-saws and especially crayons and paper. When he started Playgroup he was always on his own and it hurt so much to see him. I spent many hours trying to get away from people to cry. Put in this situation, my personal struggles showed up starkly. I couldn't be perfect, so I felt a failure and depression tried to get a hold.

Time went by and Ruth, our daughter, was born in June 1971. I had really wanted a daughter this time. She was late arriving and weighed in at 10 lbs! My doctor said to me, 'I would be careful if I were you, they get bigger!'

When Paul was four years old, Barry two and Ruth just born, we felt it was right for us to move out of the hostel situation. We wanted to spend our time with the children and there was always competition for our attention from the other members of the household. It was necessary by then for us to be on our own as a family unit. So in 1972 we moved to another house in the same town with a bigger garden for the children to play in.

Through these years we became more aware of Paul's difficulties. Having been released from the weekly visit to the Orthoptist, he was now having to have speech therapy every week, until he objected and we let things quieten down for a while.

With all these pressures on me, life was becoming unbearable and the way through the next day seemed impossible. By this time Paul had started school and Barry was at Playgroup. I had to fight back the tears at our first Parent and Teachers' evening when we went to discuss Paul's progress. The teacher, Mrs. Elliot, a lovely caring lady, told us of Paul's frustration and how he had put big lines through his friends' work through the total frustration of not even being able to hold a pencil properly. She said, 'He is a bright boy and can discuss many subjects, but he has a terrible learning/

language difficulty'. So began a new wave of problems that battered us over many years.

One particular week I finally reached the end of my tether. My head had been aching for so long and I was worried about taking any more Paracetamol tablets. I just didn't know how I was going to cope. What with Andy's demanding job with Social Services, Paul becoming more and more frustrated and Barry and Ruth growing so quickly. It's strange really, but so many people would come to me for counselling, so many parents who felt I had life sorted out, quite unaware of my feelings of inferiority. In the end I had so many mums and toddlers visiting me that I started a playgroup in the local church because this allowed them to meet each other and took the pressure off me.

Well, my headache got worse and I remember walking up and down our lounge and shouting to God, 'If you're really interested in me you have got to take my headache away'. To my amazement, it went. The next day I got out of bed and my head was sore to touch, even my hair was sensitive, and I could feel this headache hovering over me again. As I got the children off to school and playgroup, and Andy off to work, I started to cry. I didn't want this headache. It really immobilised me. Once again I cried to God, 'Please don't let this headache come back' and so clearly He answered me. Into my mind came these words, 'I can take away your headache but I want to heal what is causing it'. My life had been spent looking for acceptance, trying to find out what was bugging me. Then into my mind came a memory of my mum and myself in the hallway of the council house we had lived in before I was five years old. I had thought about it before but never, never told anyone as it was really painful. I was a toddler, being naughty as toddlers are sometimes and my mum was taking her coat from under the stairs and saying to me, 'If you're a naughty girl, I will leave you and not love you anymore'. Because my mum was under pressure at this time, she was playing the tape that had been played to her by her mum. It's an interesting thing that I could remember very little of my childhood. Only moving house and having a dog called Patch-eyed Pete, also bangs when the bombs would explode and my parents saying it was Uncle Tony making the bangs! I had blocked out everything else. For the rest of the day I felt really sick, I had never admitted this memory to myself.

When Andy came home from work and I had got the children off to bed, I said, 'Andy, I must talk to you.' He was watching TV and reading the newspaper. He didn't really want to listen. He was used to me nagging and condemning him. So I switched off the TV and said, 'Andy, you really must listen to me.' Reluctantly he put down his newspaper as I began to tell him about this memory with my mum. Even as I told him I felt like vomiting, and sobbed and sobbed great deep sobs while I got it all out. Then I curled up on his knee like a little child. I felt so empty, as if an operation had just been performed. After this, another memory followed very quickly, and this also caused great pain. It might have been on the same occasion or a different one, I don't know. I only know that I had received it as 'Truth' and taken it into my being. My mum hadn't really meant it, it was one of those tapes again! It was the same house but we were in the living room. I must have been naughty again and I was standing in the doorway with my mum sitting down. She was saying to me, 'If you're a naughty girl, I will send you to the childrens' home and get another little girl.' For all these years I had felt that if I wasn't good enough I would be replaced. Again I sobbed and sobbed, I think it was about two hours in all. I felt as if a great big 'thing' had been taken out of my inside.

It took many weeks before I realised what had happened and the effect it would have on our marriage and family. I regret that I didn't allow my emotions to be touched earlier because this experience released so much trust, joy and acceptance in our lives. It is so good this happened when it did, because somehow I was freed from the 'Parent Statement Tapes', to being loved, accepted and secure just as I was. This gave me the ability to help Paul in his difficulties in school and in his life in general. Also I was able to feed into our children's lives positive attitudes, especially to Paul who was at such a disadvantage. At this time I learned that children with specific learning/language difficulties need to have confidence built into them. They need to know they are loved and accepted unconditionally. I would encourage any parent of children under five years of age to spend time and listen to their little ones. Put your arms around them (boys as well as girls), love them and tell them you love them, even when they are naughty. Speak honestly and positively to them and don't compare them. This all takes time and energy but it is really worth while and will lead your children into a lifetime of security. And it will do lovely things for you as parents also.

A poem Ruth wrote, aged eleven years:

ACCEPTANCE
Truth, Joy, Love,
These three,
Plus acceptance of God
And acceptance of me
Are all so easy . . .
Yet hard to achieve
At moments it's even
Hard to believe
There is this Thing,
This Lamb, this God,
Who keeps us alive
And helps us plod
On through the days
Of hardship and pain,
The days of sun,
The days of rain.

Oh! Wonderful day,
When I realise God's plan
And that God loves me
Just as I am!

For all these years I had striven to be accepted, I tried my very, very best but it did not work. Somehow, in my desperation, when I could do nothing else, God performed this operation. I can't understand it fully but I know it happened because of the effect on our lives.

3

A Hidden Handicap

AS A DEVOTED PARENT I was very aware of the milestones in our children's lives. Following Dr. Spock was not my favourite pastime but I wanted our children to develop normally. It was very important to Andy and me that we didn't pressurise them into what we thought they should be, but right from birth we attempted to build up their self-esteem so that they felt wanted, loved and accepted totally as they were. We wanted from the depth of our beings for them to be secure, happy people. I loved babies and wanted everything to be right and lovely but as you know no baby is perfect in every way. They develop at such different rates and just when you are impressing somebody with how good your baby is at eating, he deposits his dinner plate on top of his head with great glee!

Paul had lots of positive input into his life from ourselves and from other members of the extended family but as we look back we can also see negative inputs that must have affected Paul's earlier life. We did our very best to nurture and protect our little ones, but as parents we don't always realise the mistakes we make. The experience with Paul's eye and the resultant operation had been a real shock to me. Of course, once that was behind us we hoped everything would become normal. But clearly this was not so.

Although Paul had started Playgroup at three years old, it was very local and probably had the cheapest fees in town. Beaconsfield is a very affluent place but at this time we were quite poor, so it was mainly out of convenience but also this playgroup was all we could afford. He enjoyed the playing but sadly as I look back I can see the rigidity of it. For Barry and Ruth we chose a much more play orientated group rather than such an organised one. Right from this early stage Paul rejected jigsaws, shapes, and using crayons and pencils. He enjoyed painting with a great sheet of paper and large brush – when I say painting I mean splashing the paint all over the paper! But he was always on his own and always appeared on the edge of things. It was difficult for him to take part in physical activities, his co-ordination was so bad and his speech so hard to understand.

From there he went to his first school in Jordans. We were recommended to this school and liked the village atmosphere. It seemed ideal as there were only about sixteen children in each class. We felt this was so necessary for Paul who was already facing difficulties. Mrs. Elliott, his first class teacher, was a lovely lady, she really gave herself to these little ones. There follows a report Mrs. Elliott has written about Paul in those early days:

> My earliest recollections of Paul go back to the day when he first came to the Village School where I was the teacher in charge of the reception class. The family did not live in the village, but his mother knew of the school through a friend of hers whose daughter was in my class at that time.
>
> The Village School catered for roughly a hundred children. There were four teachers and so it was possible to keep all the classes at a reasonable teaching level. It was a happy school and the children attending it had the opportunity to develop freely. As the classes were small

there was time to ensure that each child had his fair amount of individual attention.

Paul was a very happy, friendly little fellow with a big smile. He started school at the beginning of the term with a group of boys classed as rising fives. He had no problems in making friends and quite soon he settled into the routine of school life. His early play was imaginative and creative, and he was keen to be involved in any kind of class activity.

The first term passed happily enough for Paul and I had no reason to believe that he would experience any kind of difficulty in keeping up with other children in the group when the time came to start the basic work for reading and writing. He had a very good command of language and was able to express himself very well indeed.

Soon after the start of Paul's second term at school I began to see that he was having problems with any kind of set task that involved recalling and recording letter shapes, although I noticed that he seemed to hear the sounds given to letter shapes and could repeat them for me. All children coming into school at that time were given a medical examination and I made a note to ensure that special attention would be given to Paul's hearing and sight testing. Nothing abnormal was found and Paul was said to be a normal healthy five year old.

In spite of my efforts to give as much extra time to Paul as I could, he did not appear to be making any progress with his reading or writing.

I think at the start of his third term Paul was already beginning to sense that something the other children in the class found reasonably easy to do, he found very difficult, in fact almost impossible. He tried – how he tried – but it was no use, he just could not use the clues I gave him to help him read and write. He was so anxious to please and I felt quite sure that he was a very intelligent little boy, but how could I help him towards being able, one day, to use this intelligence? My main concern was that he should not reject himself or feel that he was on the outside of the group. I had to ensure that other tasks he achieved in were made the most of and brought to the notice of other children.

Extra remedial help was not easy to arrange for children of Paul's age and it was not until his seventh birthday that Paul's reading problem would have been brought to the notice of the school psychological service as a child who was experiencing a learning problem.

My own experience of teaching children who had a specific learning problem was at that time quite limited. The word 'dyslexic' had only recently been mentioned in educational establishments and few ordinary teachers, including myself, were quite sure what it was all about. It was a subject for discussion in the staffroom. I knew that if Paul was to make progression in these early stages of learning to read he must in no way lose confidence in himself. Work in the classroom with the other children must continue to be fun, stimulating and interesting. There must be an exciting motivating environment that would foster his interest in learning to read. Many children who experience difficulties in their learning programme become naughty and make a nuisance of themselves in the classroom. Paul was not like this – I never remember him creating a disturbance in the class, only how very hard he tried to come to terms with his problem.

It was this plucky determination that made me want to help him in any way I could. So I set about working out a phonic programme for Paul based on his auditory capability which he seemed to be more at ease with.

Paul's mother was well aware of his difficulty and most concerned to help in any way she could. Continuous repetitive teaching was, I felt, essential so during school holidays, and whenever it was possible, Paul came to my home for extra help. We built up a very close relationship but unfortunately just at this time when we were beginning to make some progress Paul's family had to move house and this meant that he would have to attend a much larger school. This would be a very difficult step for him as the new school had many more children attending it. He would miss his friends and the security of the small village school.

My interest in Paul and my admiration for his courage, which kept him trying afresh every day, made we want to find out more about other children who were highly intelligent and yet had a learning problem. It was after my trial and error experience with Paul and others like him that I went on to further educational training which enabled me eventually to run a unit for these children. If Paul could have benefited from such a unit is his early days at school perhaps reading and writing would not have been such a painful experience for him over such a long period.'

At our first parents evening as we were all congregated in the hall, Mr. Dwight, the headteacher, spoke of the future of these little ones and how he wanted them to adjust happily to school life. Then Mrs. Elliott spoke about how to motivate children to learn and explained some of the problems they would face. Then she said, 'I'm sure Mr. and Mrs. Croall won't mind me saying this but last week Paul put two great big lines across his partner's book, he is experiencing such frustration. It wasn't naughtiness. He was experiencing such frustration because he was incapable of doing work like the other children.' She was wanting other parents to be understanding of this situation but it hurt so much, not that she had drawn attention to it but that there was such a frustration in Paul. My heart sank; I loved this kid so much, what could be done to help him?

At the end of the session she came and apologised for using Paul as an example but said, 'I know he is an intelligent boy but is facing such difficulties. I would like to help him to overcome his difficulties.' For the next two terms, and through the holidays she took Paul to her home and gave him an individual lesson free of charge. She was so caring and found it hard to see him struggle so. We are grateful to her for spending time and energy and giving of her expertise in those very early years.

At the end of his first year Mrs. Elliott was moving on to another school to take up a headship and, as this coincided with us moving house, we moved Paul to our local First School. Had Mrs. Elliott been continuing to teach Paul we would have kept him at Jordans School and transported him from our new home. On saying good-bye to Mrs. Elliott, she asked us to keep in touch with her and let her know how Paul fared in his 'O' levels. She said 'I know Paul is an intelligent boy and I would love to be kept in touch with his progress.'

It was from this school in 1973 that Paul was referred by his headmaster and speech therapist, to the School Medical Officer. At that time he felt Paul's problem was purely emotional as some of these learning/ language difficulties can have an emotional basis, but you can imagine I searched continually for an answer to Paul's learning difficulty and considered all the possible physical causes.

Pregnancy?
Mercury poisoning?
Squint at eighteen months?

Continual eye testing?
Eye operation at two plus years?
Emotional pressure from extended family

Firstly I considered my pregnancy, which was a very happy time, it was exciting planning for this little one. Things happened at this time that might have been a possible cause, but we will never know. What we do know is that God gave us Paul exactly as he was and made us responsible for his care and development. It has made such an impression on our lives as a family that we thank God for this time. There has been heartache and pain, but it has been mixed with much joy and rejoicing. My mind was similar to a computer, it kept on checking out different avenues of what could have happened. Why did Paul have to suffer so? Was it a minimal brain dysfunction? Was it his vision? But what caused it? I pondered, was the Debendox for early morning sickness responsible? Or when at twenty-four weeks into my pregnancy I had a very nasty fall which gave me a hard knock across my abdomen and severe shock, and I was sedated for two days. Was that the cause?

I also considered the possibility of mercury poisoning. For many years I had worked as a Dental Surgery Assistant/Dental Health Educator, which often meant working with mercury. When I first worked in a dental surgery in Liverpool it was standard practice to mix mercury with your bare hands. Research has shown that the vapour from the mercury can cause poisoning to the system. An article in the Sunday Observer recently suggested that mercury poisoning could be responsible for stillbirths, cot deaths, and handicaps of children. It is being fully researched at the moment. Could this be a root? My mind raced backwards and forwards over every possible cause; we will never know exactly, but I do know that God's way is perfect, He doesn't make mistakes.

It was from this situation that Paul was first referred to the School Medical Officer, in June 1973, when he was six years old. Children with a whole range of difficulties are referred to this person, generally by the teacher or doctor or sometimes at the request of the parent. The teacher may have observed a child under-achieving, or struggling in a certain area and he or she may feel that this particular child could benefit from extra input at school or home.

So we were given an appointment with Dr. Burne, the School Medical Officer for the Beaconsfield and Amersham area. He visited us at our home. Andy had worked alongside Dr. Burne on occasions, so it was an unusual situation we encountered. He was a big man and very charming. I would think at medical aspects excellent but this one baffled him. Does the doctor really understand? He wanted to understand, but here was an attractive child with 'normal' parents, able to verbalise on many subjects, yet unable even to hold a pencil. Was it a medical problem?

Dr. Burne wanted to help. But what could he do? There was nothing he could prescribe, no drugs would heal this one. We realised it was going to be a real hard struggle but we would do everything possible to help Paul. We chatted together in our lounge, Dr. Burne, Andy, Paul and myself. We talked about pregnancy, eye operation, speech defect, and we explained that Paul experienced difficulty in holding a pencil, catching a ball, kicking a ball, reading or writing. We talked about our extended family, as we wondered whether Paul's problem was purely emotional. Dr. Burne thought this seemed to be the only answer.

For many years children who have had a learning/language problem, have been labelled as 'not trying', 'lazy', 'not attentive', or 'badly behaved'. Word blindness has been around for many, many years, or children 'who reverse letters'. Within the last ten years much research has been done into Dyslexia or reading/writing/language difficulties. Even as I write, the media has revealed new advances in understanding and tackling these problems. For example, if a child is given particular eye exercises it will help to mature the muscle, which to some extent will enable the child to see without the letters and figures moving around. Also a child can now be given particular glasses with a frosted lens, which will help to correct this movement which is so frustrating when trying to focus.

Dr. Eileen Watkins told me how she felt so inadequate as there was nothing medically that she could do. Her report stated that Paul was:

> A child who would never be able to express himself in writing, but I felt because of his parents he was superbly confident and would get on in the world somehow, but would never do anything academically. I was desperately unhappy for him, for he had a handicap that medicine could not heal.

Dr. Eileen explained to me that she was hoping that Dr. Burne might have diagnosed a minor brain dysfunction, but his report was quite honest: he didn't really know too much about this area of difficulty. He said to Andy and me, 'You probably have more understanding of this area than I do.'

You may be a parent of a child with a handicap, which could simply be as a habit that embarrasses you, like nail biting or thumb sucking. Or it could be something that restricts the child's emotional and physical life, such as Dyslexia, bad eyesight, deafness, blindness, mental handicap, Down's syndrome, epilepsy, spasticity or deformed body, or being bound to a wheel chair as a result of an accident. There are many, many more handicaps. The natural feeling is that you want to protect this child. You may want to hide the difficulty because it causes you embarrassment. You feel that other people will not understand, they won't approve. It nearly breaks your heart when someone else has to look after your child, but you really can't cope much longer. Often we put on our children the things we believe people think of us – this is not always truth, it is often lies, things that have been put into our characters from an early age.

Occasionally my husband, Andy, comes home from work after spending much time and energy with a family who have a handicapped child and he weeps. It is heartbreaking to see how the parents may feel it is all their fault. They examine every detail of their lives; 'If only I hadn't done this', 'If only we had waited', 'If only I hadn't allowed Bobby to go on his bike'. Sadly they feel they have to pay for this. Have you ever seen a child who has a handicap of one kind or another who is spoilt? Mainly because of their guilt feelings, the parents give in to every whim of the child. We see it portrayed on some TV films, the child who controls all the family and household. The parents are so overcome with this child that the rest of the family feel like outsiders, as if they are not important, they always have to make allowances for this child. Sad to see, but their needs to be loved and accepted are ignored. And, of course, this can also happen to a marriage partner. It is not an easy task to bring into balance the needs of a family, but put into this complex situation a handicapped child, it can show up so many inadequacies in even a strong marriage relationship.

4

Does The Doctor Really Understand?

FROM THE SMALL SCHOOL in Jordans Paul moved on to another larger school. It was a new building, very nicely set out and one felt at ease when entering the school. It was a very free and easy atmosphere, with children working at their own pace. The headmistress was very positive about Paul and wanted to help him but, as in any school, the staff vary. Most of the teachers were also positive toward him but unfortunately one member of staff was very negative towards Paul. She told him and us that he was lazy, naughty and not trying, which was totally untrue. In the next class he really progressed, the teacher was excellent and she motivated him to want to overcome his difficulties.

The building of this new school, which the children transferred to at eight years old, backed onto the First School grounds. It was generally a natural transition for the children from one to the other but this school was, nevertheless, very different. The whole approach was of authoritarian-type teaching, with great emphasis put upon reading and writing. If the child was unable to read or write they were immediately a failure. My husband telephoned the school head, to be told that 'we judge the children only by their reading ability'. Lists of the achievements and failure of children were put up on the classroom walls for everyone to see.

There was no way we could let Paul face this. He would be a failure before he started.

We enquired about other schools in the area but at that time it was not so easy to get a child into a school outside your catchment area. However, when the headmistress of the First School called for Andy and me, we felt we had no choice but to fight all we could for Paul to go to a school where teachers and head were sympathetic. She said to us, 'It is difficult for me to say this but if Paul was my son I wouldn't let him go into this local school. I have a son who is now twenty-six years old and still suffering from this type of education. He was very like Paul'. So we really didn't have a choice. We telephoned, wrote letters, did everything possible to get around the red tape of the education system. It was hard work but very worthwhile.

The result of all this was that in September 1975 Paul moved to Butlers Court Middle School, which was about one and a half miles from our home. We faced the problem that his friends would be going to the local school but we involved Paul in the choice and he felt it was better for him to be able to learn at his own pace. His first teacher at the new school was Mrs. Stevenson, who wrote this report, dated 23rd April 1976 to the psychologist:

> Paul has been in my class since September 1975 during which time he has also had extra reading practice daily with the head remedial teacher.
>
> It was obvious from the beginning that he is a very immature child for his age. This is shown in his physical movements, his speech, his written work and his difficulty in learning to read.
>
> His speech tends to be very babyish, although he sometimes uses very good vocabulary and shows good logical thinking. His written work is very limited and his letter formations are more like those of a five-year-old than an eight plus.

Paul's reading gradually improved during the two terms he has been with us as he gained more confidence in recognising letters and being able to build the word phonetically. This, however, is only after he has been given much time in daily reading practice and even then his progress is very slow.

Paul has quite good number concept up to 20. He is quite conversant with +, −, x, with numbers up to 100, but is unable to do addition with carrying figures. His recognition of numbers is quite good but he often writes numbers like 3 and 9 back to front.

Socially Paul does not mix in very well with the other children in the group. He seems to prefer his own company.

(signed) K. Stevenson
Teacher

It was then that we heard of an eminent Consultant Neurologist, Dr. Macdonald Critchley. Dr. Critchley had carried out a tremendous amount of research into children with learning/language difficulties. He had also written many books on Dyslexia aimed at helping teachers, parents and children suffering from this handicap.

After discussing the matter with Dr. Eileen Watkins she kindly referred us to Dr. Critchley for diagnosis, and the wheels began to turn. Prior to the appointment there was a large questionnaire to be completed, asking about family history, pregnancy, and illnesses. We filled this in and then waited until we received an appointment.

It was an exciting day for Paul travelling up to London to Dr. Critchley's consulting rooms, while other children were at school. We wondered if the interview was going to be an ordeal but Dr. Critchley was a pleasant man and Paul was at ease from the word 'go'. He had never had difficulty in verbalising what was in his mind, in fact it had been his only way of communicating his thoughts and ideas. Paul happily spend an hour with this gentleman on his own. Afterwards, Dr. Critchley spoke to Andy and me. He told us what we already knew, that Paul had great difficulty and needed help.

This letter was sent to Dr. Eileen after our consultation:

3rd May, 1976.

Dear Dr. Watkins,

Thank you very much for asking me to see your patient Paul Croall and for your full and helpful letter about him. I am returning the letter from the School Medical Officer which you so kindly allowed me to study.

Paul has certainly improved in many respects but he still shows many signs of immaturity as for example in his speech and in his spontaneous drawings. He is behindhand with reading and spelling, and he confessed to me that he cannot copy quickly enough from a blackboard to get all his work down on paper. On the other hand, arithmetic presents far less in the way of difficulties.

Paul's handwriting, both spontaneous and in copying, is big, sprawling, with ill-formed letters and the handwriting itself is executed with undue slowness. His spontaneous writing of numerals and letters shows reversals and he tends frequently to draw numerals and letters from below upwards.

I found that Paul's present reading age is only 7.06 (and he read with extreme slowness) and his spelling age is less than seven, his chronological age being just nine.

I would regard Paul as being dyslextic but whether his Dyslexia is of the 'developmental' type, I am not sure. His father confessed that he himself had been a late reader, but he has no problems now and no one else in the family is a poor or reluctant reader or an erratic speller.

Paul's Dyslexia might conceivably be the expression of a minimal brain dysfunction. In favour of this is the history of a squint, and of an earlier speech defect. Furthermore, Paul is still rather clumsy and I found him inordinately slow in the execution of spatio-constructional tasks, as well as in reading and writing. His spontaneous drawings are immature. There is no trace of crossed laterality.

Whatever the precise type of Paul's Dyslexia I am confident he would be helped if only he could receive some extra help on a one-to-one basis at the hands of some teacher who is experienced in dealing with Dyslexics. I know that there are more than one such persons with suitable qualifications in your area and Mrs. Croall believes she could find someone suitable.

Meanwhile I will write to the Headmaster of Butler's Court School telling him what I think about Paul's problem, asking him to co-operate in making these extra lessons feasible.

Yours sincerely,
(signed) Dr. Macdonald Critchley

After our visit to Dr. Macdonald Critchley we realised that generally educationalists don't like the finality of the word 'Dyslexic' but refer to 'a child with a Specific Learning/Language difficulty'. They feel that 'Dyslexic' can be used as an umbrella trying to cover many learning difficulties and, as such, is not helpful in indicating which particular teaching approaches will help the child. Also 'Dyslexic' can be used as a label and encourage the child to opt out and not work towards overcoming his difficulty. So don't worry too much if your psychologist's hair stands on end when you mention the word 'Dyslexia'. He is wanting a clearer definition of the child's learning problem. We found it helped Paul to know that his problem was not of 'being stupid' or 'not trying' or being 'lazy'. To be honest, we didn't mind what it was called, we just wanted him to be helped and this came from Mr. Norman, the Educational Psychologist. He liaised with the school and initially arranged that Paul should have four lessons a week with a remedial teacher, Mrs. Dell. She was such a gracious lady, so patient and yet so able to get Paul motivated to read and write although there were big obstacles in the way.

The following is a report written by Mr. Norman from the notes he made at the time:

> PAUL CROALL, d.o.b. 4.4.67
> Seen at Cheena House, 28.5.76
> Paul is an attractive, fair-haired lad, who appeared at ease from the beginning of the session. His speech is immature in its articulation and he pronounces many words with a rather odd, flattened vowel sound. This is accounted for in part by his parents' regional accent. His linguistic skills are still poor and on occasions, he misunderstood questions that I asked him. He presents as a lively, alert and chatty child, who obviously enjoys school and I did not detect any underlying anxieties. On the contrary, at times it was difficult to break-in on his conversation, as he talked about his inventions, including a lightning conductor to help drive the electricity in his house and various plans he had for wells. It was difficult to keep up with the flow of ideas, despite his relatively poor fluency for speech.
>
> His drawings are immature, both in their form and perception. Paper and pencil skills are weak and he writes slowly, with little fluency and with many of the letter shapes being incorrectly

formed. He applies a great deal of pressure to the paper when writing, which causes him to tire quickly. He has now developed consistent laterality but I understand that he only settled on his right hand for most tasks when he was about six-and-a-half years old. This strongly suggests the possibility of visual perceptual problems, as we know from recent research, that uncertain laterality can lead to confusions over reversals and inversions. On tasks presented from the Wechsler Intelligence Scale for Children, he functioned erratically. On the Verbal Scale he gained a below average score on the Information Sub-Test and bearing in mind that he comes from a verbal and stimulating home background, it seems highly likely that he has difficulty retrieving facts from his memory. In contrast, on the remaining sub-tests he gained good average and above average scaled scores, reflecting his better ability to cope with tasks involving verbal reasoning and number skills. On the Additional Sub-Test of Digit Span which taps short-term memory and audiatory sequencing ability, he gained an average score.

On items from the Performance Scale, again his scale score ranged from the below average to the above average. He did particularly poorly on the Coding Sub-Test, which involves eye, hand co-ordination skills and visual matching abilities.

His reading lacks fluency and he appears to be bound on the phonic approach. He is able to use context cues in some circumstances but has a very limited visual vocabulary. He knows the letter sounds fairly well but there are still some areas of uncertainty. He is able to consistently synthesize three and four letter words and copes well with consonant blends and three letter clusters. He knows the consonant digraphs 'ch' ‘sh’ and ‘th’ and copes with the final ‘e’ rule. He now needs further help in developing the ability to break down and build up multi-syllabic words and exercises to develop his knowledge of the vowel digraphs. He copes least well with his visual vocabulary and I have discussed a variety of ways which can be used to improve this, including work involving the flash card sequence and a multi-sensory approach. To help him with his spelling, I would also recommend a multi-sensory approach to encourage the use of as many sensory modalities as possible. He continues to require language work to extend his expressive language skills and comprehension ability and the use of Cloze material, would be of benefit to him in this area.

His reproduction of the designs from the Graham Kendal Test do not show any gross visual perceptual confusions but do suggest that his ability to reproduce shapes from memory, is poorly developed. This has implications on how he will cope with copying from the blackboard.

Future Objectives:
It will be necessary to discuss in some depth, with Mrs. Dell, Remedial Teacher at Butler’s Court School, Paul’s educational needs and areas where he requires support. At present his phonic skills are the stronger part of his reading strategies and he needs help to extend his visual vocabulary, improve his fluency for reading and encourage his ability to use context cues. At the present time, he appears to be reading solely to please the listener and work must aim at making reading a more pleasurable experience for him and to help him derive meaning from what he reads.

P. F. Norman,
Senior Educational Psychologist

Mrs. Dell has written her account of her meeting with Paul and his work standard at the time:

> I well remember when Paul joined my reading class at Butlers Court School. He had a twinkle in his eye, a smile on his lips and plenty to say. He didn't like reading aloud and he disliked writing even more. Paul was an unusual boy but, in our small group, he got on well with his peers.
>
> Paul's reading was slow and laboured which could be frustrating for him. He would confuse the order of syllables in a word, confuse 'b' and 'd' and miss out small words. He did listen to what he was reading and he knew if the text sounded nonsensical. Paul's good natured sense of humour was always an asset – for the teacher as well. He would greatly enjoy trying to prove the author wrong – especially in science books. Given the slightest encouragement, Paul would embark on a lively discussion in preference to reading aloud.
>
> I felt that Paul was not reading words in their natural sequence – from left to right. His handwriting action was poorly co-ordinated and, not surprisingly, his spelling was very poor. Paul's knowledge of phonetics was good so we built on this and incorporated the 'Look and Say' method with flash cards, dictionary work and many reading games. The reading schemes we used were 1) The Rescue Series and 2) The Pirate Books – with many science books. Paul also used work books and did tracing exercises to give more flow and control to his pen – and many spelling techniques.
>
> In spite of his difficulties Paul did not appear to feel 'different' but he may have been more aware of this in his classroom situation. I always felt that the very sensible and supportive role of Paul's parents played a vital part in Paul's

development. He had a wide and varied vocabulary largely due to listening to stories and taking part in conversation. Paul was made to feel he had strengths to build on other than academic ones. His parents were anxious to help without making Paul feel pressurised.

'Paul is being even more successful than I would have anticipated and I wish him every success.

Betty Dell

In a report of a test Mr. Norman gave Paul at the time, he said:

> His performance and tests of intellectual ability were interesting: He performed erratically with scores ranging from below average to well above average. He had difficulty with retrieving information stores in his brain. When he was exposed to information, i.e. memory, he could not retrieve the facts.

This caused him so much frustration, and it was not an easy job for Mrs. Dell to help him through this difficult stage of development. At the end of that school year Paul's report read: 'Paul works to the best of his ability. Paul tries very hard but is progressing very slowly. He needs a lot of help both with his English and number work. He is a happy and helpful boy but he prefers his own company to that of other children.'

His next class was a very bright group being taught by Mrs. Adele Thomas. I spoke to Mrs. Thomas recently and asked what her memories were of Paul:

> I remember him as a small rather timid nine-year-old. He was intelligent but uncoordinated. He had a sparkle, and was always keen to chat. He had difficulty relating to his peers primarily because of his lack of coordination. He could

never kick a ball and children noticed that he was different and that he found school work difficult. It wasn't easy for Paul as he wasn't really accepted. He preferred to talk to adults and I learnt so much about his family and was thrilled that they were Christians.

Paul was the first real case of Dyslexia I had come across. He confused many letters and wrote things back to front. He had great difficulty with reading, writing and spelling. I remember once asking the children to draw the picture in their mind after listening to 'The Promenade Music'. Once the picture was drawn the next stage was to write the story of the picture. Paul couldn't get his ideas down on paper, so he told me them instead. He showed great imagination and perception (as good as some of the most imaginative in the class and many had very high IQ's). It was this that made me first realise how intelligent Paul was. I wanted desperately to help him and studied books on Dyslexia to that end. I spent as much time as I could giving him attention but nowhere near enough. His progress was painfully slow and I felt totally inadequate to deal with the problem.

As for the school, they were concerned but powerless to do anything: there was always such a shortage of money. The staff had a genuine concern and were caring but in the State system powerless. He needed more than just four half-hour sessions per week on an individual basis. The frustration Paul must have felt at times must have been great, yet he never showed it. I felt that God's hand was truly on him in spite of his handicap, there was something very endearing and very loving about him. His general knowledge surprised and baffled us all. He remembered everything he was being taught but could not put it down on paper.

As a teacher I felt my main role was to encourage and praise him as much as possible and try to make him feel 'special' in spite of his handicap. I had to accept on one hand that what I could do was limited but on the other what I knew God could do one day was without limits.

I remember Paul having a great depth of spirituality, he never complained about others and he showed considerable discernment in situations. Time after time Paul asked me to start a Christian Union in the school. At the time it was not possible but later, after Paul left the school, circumstances changed and I was able to do this. It was Paul who put the idea into my mind and it was through him that I began a group in my school.

In spite of his Dyslexia I felt that Paul would succeed eventually. Personally, I felt inadequate to help him as much as I would have liked to, but looking back I can see God's hand in all of this. Through Paul's handicap and God's intervention to heal him in his own time many people have been, and will be, blessed and helped.

5

Early School Years

BY MARCH 1976, when Paul was still nine years old, his problem was becoming more obvious – especially as his brother and sister, Barry and Ruth, were so quick at reading and writing. Like everyone else we led busy lives and time was so short but somehow we made time to read with the children at bedtime. It wasn't always easy and some days we would be exhausted. Paul, Barry and Ruth would especially enjoy 'Dad' reading to them. It was a necessity to read to Paul but also so important for Barry and Ruth. We learned how essential it is for parents to spend time with their children, to listen to them and communicate with them. There will never be a time like this again. Andy and I were in demand from many people but we knew that God had given us our kids, exactly as they were. He knew the problems and difficulties, but we are responsible to lead and teach them and this doesn't just happen, it takes time and effort.

The headteacher and staff were very good. Each term they held a case conference with the headteacher, class teacher, remedial teacher, psychologist and ourselves. They were all so interested in Paul's progress and doing everything possible to help. But we still had questions that never seemed to be answered. Couldn't God have just answered our prayers without all this hassle? But He didn't and we had to go through it day after day, week after week, term after term and year after year seeking help from all the sources available.

People have come to us for counsel and we have looked at their attitudes and at their hang-ups, and then have advised them to seek help from the School Psychological Service not only for their family's sake but also for their own. Some have been quite put out by our suggestion but it has been with a hint of glee that I have retorted 'We have seen the Educational Psychologist for many years with Paul'. Somehow they feel that Andy and I must be different, that we have it all together. This is true in one way because we are so sure that God is for us and is on our side, but this doesn't mean that we will avoid heartache and pain, but that we don't have to face it alone, and that whatever happens in our lives, God will work it for our good. We have taught and encouraged our children that in all situations God is for us, He isn't against us. We have tried to encourage them to have a thankful heart and that life isn't always fair. We have tried to convey to Paul, Barry and Ruth that we love them all equally, but in some circumstances it appears as if things are not fair. It has to be like that sometimes. Paul would look at his difficulties, he would be sad at negative remarks, but his attitude was that of thankfulness in spite of his circumstances. He was attending Butlers Court Middle School at this time, and finding things rather hard.

One day the telephone rang; it was the secretary from the school. She said, 'Sorry, Mrs. Croall, but Paul is not at all well, he is lying on the bench in the hallway; could you collect him?' I was without a car at that time, so it took a little time for me to ring around and borrow one from a friend. On arriving in the hall of the school, I found Paul looking rather flushed but so happy. He explained, 'Mum, my head was hurting so much, it was really sore, so I did what grandad Rowlands told me, that is to thank God for everything, even my headache. As I lay on the bench I began to sing and thank God for my headache and I just began singing in another language that God could understand.' Here was a child experiencing such difficulty with the English language and yet spontaneously singing in a new language. This may be something completely new to you but it is spoken of in the Bible as a gift of the Holy Spirit which God gives to His church.

Our next meeting with Mr. Norman, the Educational Psychologist, was at our home. I think he probably wanted to see the whole family in relationship together, and to assess the home environment. Paul, Barry and Ruth were very excited at this gentleman coming to our home and they had lots of things to show him. Ruth had her pretty dress on, Barry his new football boots as he wanted to show how he could kick a ball – just like Kevin Keegan! Paul had great ideas about being an inventor, he had talked to Mr. Norman about this previously. He had some excellent ideas and would spend hours drawing detailed plans of these ideas, but he was often the only one who could understand them! I found this example of Paul's writing when he was nine and a half years old:

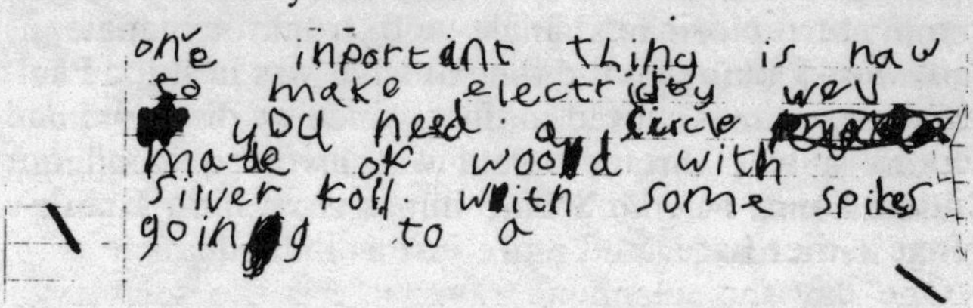
one inportant thing is haw
to make electridey wev
you need a circle
made of wood with
silver foil with some spikes
going to a

Before Mr. Norman arrived Paul had been working on a new invention, it was a lightning conductor. He was going to supply electricity for the whole house. His ideas was to attract the lightning to his conductor (a car aerial). On the end of the conductor he had a long wire with a three-pin plug attached. Fortunately he did not try this experiment until we had congregated in the lounge. He stood outside the patio door beckoning Mr. Norman to take the plug and put it in the socket! He was so proud but could have done himself some damage. Andy gently explained to him that his idea was good, especially if it saved us money on our electricity bill, but one had to check with an adult before carrying out experiments with electricity! His mind was constantly working out these plans and inventions.

Speaking from my position as a parent relating to the Educational Psychologist I saw an interwoven relationship, each person being an individual but working in a continuum, e.g:

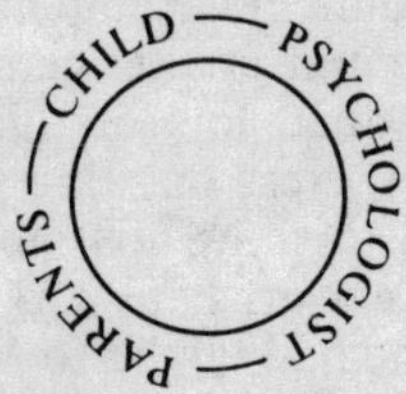

It was not one against the other as in conflict – but it was a close circle, constantly moving, frequently reassessing our aims and objectives, from Paul's angle, from Mr. Norman's angle and from our angle as parents, looking all the time at what was best for Paul. This sometimes caused conflict, which we discussed and found a way through. Paul was involved in all our discussions, we didn't hide things from him. I realise that if we had related more just as individuals, e.g:

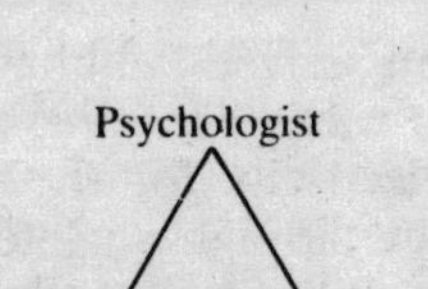

we might have had clearer directions of a more authoritarian type but not assessing the whole situation so clearly. The way we tackled it, the circle approach, took more time and energy and we all had to be more flexible, but I believe we achieved our objectives without losing too much on the way. Our working relationship with this particular Educational Psychologist was very good but psychologists vary, as do parents, teachers and children.

Many parents do not know that you can refer directly to the Educational Psychologist. It had always appeared to me that referrals had to be made via the school but this is not the case. You may be faced with a teacher or headteacher who doesn't really wish to accept or understand that a child can have a learning difficulty or who views you as just a fussy parent. You have the freedom to contact the School Psychological Service and the school need not know. Of course, the psychologist may ask your permission to talk to the headteacher about your child, but if you feel you are up against a negative attitude in the school, you can explain this to the psychologist.

It was after our consultation with Dr. Macdonald Critchley that the school headteacher referred Paul to the School Psychologist. Talking to other parents it has amazed me that so many feel very negative about the psychologist. They feel that there is a stigma attached as if they are mad or not coping with pressure. We were in a unique situation with Andy being an Assistant Director of Social Services and involved in so many child care crises every day. Many people would come to Andy and me for counsel on marriage, family relationships, emotional and spiritual problems, and yet here we were putting ourselves into the hands of an Educational Psychologist. We had avoided getting too many people involved in Paul's life as we had not wanted to expose him unnecessarily and to avoid him feeling he was so different to other children. We didn't want him to be labelled, but as he was getting older it became more difficult to progress without professional help.

In June 1976 we had a case conference at the school attended by the Headteacher, Paul, the class teacher, the remedial teacher, the psychologist and ourselves. This first case conference I found very, very difficult. The whole range of problem areas were strewn across in front of us. My heart sank, I felt a big lump in my throat and my eyes filled up with tears. It's easier to be objective when the problem belongs to someone else but this was my son being discussed. I wanted to run out of that room and not face the pain, but deep within me I knew that if Paul was to be helped to work at his difficulties my own feelings had to be controlled. Somehow we had to trust these educationalists and psychologist with our child.

November 1976, Paul again visited Mr. Norman; his main difficulty at this time was copying from the blackboard, it was practically impossible for him to do so. Mr. Norman wrote to the school to advise. A further case conference followed in the December. His teacher, Mrs. Thomas, thought he was a very isolated child but had a certain charisma about him.

The years when Paul was nine to ten years old were probably the hardest years to face. The prospect was inevitably daunting. To fit into a state educational system where children have to have reached a certain standard at particular times brought us little hope or comfort. The feelings we faced when it was reported 'his progress has slowed down'. We felt that actually meant it had stopped, because his progress was always very, very slow. This was one of our very darkest moments. We had done everything possible to help Paul. We had seen the doctor, the consultant, the psychologist, the teachers, and we had had special remedial help at home. We had also tried to help his co-ordination. This posed a big problem because this difficulty put him outside the many and varied sporting activities that his few friends enjoyed. Swimming he enjoyed but time was limited with three children. It was a major effort to get them to the next town to the swimming pool. We did it but it took another half day. Constantly we had to weigh all our priorities. We needed as a family to look at every situation. We didn't want to devote all our time and energy to Paul and allow Ruth and Barry to become outsiders. They were equally as important as Paul. As Ruth grew she became very keen on gymnastics, which meant a weekly trip to the Sports Centre. It worked well as Barry and Paul could go swimming while Ruth excelled on the bars and ropes in the gymnasium. Both Barry and Ruth were keen on music and they had piano lessons for some time. Barry was also learning to play the guitar and Ruth the clarinet. We encouraged Paul to have a go at playing the trumpet for a very short time, but the energy it took him to look at a sheet of music was an immediate 'put off'. We also looked at all the possibilities of Paul becoming involved in some social activity. We searched every avenue. How could we help his co-ordination? How could we involve him in some sport he would be able to cope with and enjoy? Team games were quite impossible.

During 1976 Andy's mother died, which was a great loss to ourselves and the children. She had been the local District Midwife in the Everton area of Liverpool and was loved by many thousands of people. Her illness had only been a short one and she passed on to be with her God and Father whom she really loved. She had worked hard all of her life but hadn't amassed great wealth, as she had always been so generous to anyone in need. But she had left the grandchildren a small sum each. At this time they were nine, seven and five years old. We had a family chat as to what the kiddies wanted to do with their money. We thought it might help to put it into the bank for them. Then thought it might help Paul's co-ordination to ride a horse as they all loved animals. They had had riding lessons from time to time and this seemed to be the answer. They all agreed that they would like a pony. We had thought of it previously but the cost was too much. Now, not really understanding what we were letting ourselves in for, off we went to the stables.

The first pony we bought was very pretty and easy to catch, but soon we discovered that he had a mind of his own. His name was Juniper. He once took Paul over a six-bar gate from stand-still. Next he decided to gallop off with me riding him. It was impossible to hold him and I ended up with fractured ribs and a lot less confidence! So we decided he had to go. We exchanged him for a 'slow old girl', called Minerva, who was very sweet. She gave us all lots of confidence. Paul, Barry and Ruth all used to ride her, until eventually Paul was getting frustrated with her as she was so slow. We again exchanged her for a 12.2 hands Dunn pony called Saxon. He had belonged to friends of ours and we knew he was pretty fast but well behaved.

By this time Barry was more interested in his new bike and Ruth was too small to be allowed on Saxon on her own. So Paul was the one who rode him and looked after him. We kept him in a field about fifty yards from our home with a number of other horses. Flippancy was his favourite companion, and they just hated to be separated. But they caused us some anxious and embarrassing moments! We were woken one morning by the sound of horse's hooves in the garden. It was about 5 a.m. We found Saxon and Flippancy had arrived and brought with them two other big horses from the field. We quickly woke the children, put on anoraks on top of our nightwear and marched them all back to the field. Saxon was so clever he could always escape. We nicknamed him Houdini-Saxon!

The school Ruth and Barry attended was about 100 yards from the field. One day during Assembly, they looked out of the window and saw Saxon and Flippancy in the school grounds eating the flowers! They thought this was great fun, it really brightened up the occasion!

Fortunately the teacher allowed them out of school to catch the ponies and take them back to the field.

On another occasion, when my mum, a real city lady, was staying with us, I was working at Chesham Dental Clinic which is about ten miles from our home. It was a very busy clinic with a long list of patients waiting to have their teeth extracted under general anaesthetic. It was all very tense and once the session got started we always ignored the telephone if it rang. That day, however, the anaesthetist was a few minutes late so I answered this one phone call. It was my mum in utter and complete panic, but also quite amused. She said, 'Saxon and Flippancy are in the front garden and I don't know what to do with them!' My heart dropped, what could I do ten miles away and just beginning this busy general anaesthetic session? We lived on quite a busy road just past a corner and on a hill! In my mind I pictured the situation, two loose horses on this road with my mum trying to catch them! Quickly I telephoned my friend Anna Carey, because we had bought Saxon from her family. Fortunately her husband, John, a local doctor, had just come home for a moment before starting his morning house calls. He didn't anticipate his first call being to two loose horses! Together John and Anna went to my mum's rescue, caught the horses and put them back into the field. Saxon and Flippancy got quite famous and once the local press phoned us and asked us for a story. They had heard of these two horses trotting around the town on their own. The headlines said 'Ponies keep hoofing it to town!'

It was three years of hard work but very worthwhile. It gave us all a lot of joy, panic and laughter. Most of all, it gave Paul a confidence which previously he didn't have. He learnt how to exercise authority and control and to shout. He had been quite a timid boy but at last he could actually do something that other children couldn't. It improved his co-ordination and helped him partake in group activities. Saxon was a fun pony but

Paul also entered him in local shows. One day he won a rosette and was so delighted. We kept Saxon until Paul's legs nearly touched the floor. Barry was not too interested and Ruth at that time was not quite strong enough for him. Eventually we sold him. The day he went it was pouring down heaven's hardest. I prayed that he would go into the horse box without any trouble, which he did. We were all there to see him off and then came home and had a cry together. It had been hard work but he had become part of the family. He had played a very important role in our family life. Even now when I see horses, I look to see if Saxon is amongst them!

6

Is This The Love Of God To Our Son?

TIME WAS PASSING so quickly. Paul was nine years old and really struggling. We were visiting the Educational Psychologist, having case conferences at school, having extra help at home, and every day he was receiving remedial help at school. His school reports were very sad. They said his conduct, helpfulness, punctuality and effort were excellent, but his actual work output was very low. His written work was practically non-existent or indecipherable. But Paul never gave up, in fact, he can remember the day when he decided that if he was going to learn he was going to have to work very, very hard. He was determined that, although the struggle was very hard, he was going to make the best of it. Not only make the best of it but he was going to beat it. He explained to me recently that the letters would go into his mind but a short time later when he learnt more letters he felt they were pushing the original ones out. Anything that he learnt just seemed to fall out again. Andy explained to him at the time that he was going to have to work a lot harder than other children of his age because of this difficulty. He remembers that his mind seemed to be divided into little compartments. When he heard information it went into a compartment, but, when he needed it again and had to recall it, there was the problem. It was as if he had a link which was missing or not functioning properly, so somehow a way had to be found of helping him to recall this information when he needed it. From that moment on, Paul was determined he was going to go into attack over this handicap. It is the first time I have heard this from him although we knew he was prepared to work hard. Andy tried to explain in simple language to Paul what was happening, which is why I want to stress the importance of communicating with your children. They love you, they trust you and want to be encouraged by you.

His life ambition was to be an inventor, he thought up the most complex machines or working models. He found it difficult to manipulate small pieces like Lego, or Meccano, but his mind was full of inventions. He would draw endless plans, but it was impossible to understand them, they appeared so bizarre. In his mind they were so straightforward. He would spend hours explaining them.

When a child has a specific learning/language difficulty it causes tremendous frustration not to be able to communicate on paper like his contemporaries. It is so necessary to listen and allow the child to explain orally what is on his mind. This is not always easy as with a mum, she may have a thousand and one other things on her mind! When Paul wanted to talk to me it couldn't wait, which was understandable because he was working out so many things in his head but couldn't write them down. Mind you, he hasn't changed much, it is usually when I am cooking supper, with guests about to arrive, that he follows me around the kitchen explaining the latest programme he has just designed for the computer! I would urge every parent to listen to your children. Don't tell them 'Children should be seen and not heard'. Make sure that you are disciplined in your life with your work, neighbours and friends. Don't allow the nagging moans of your neighbour to detract from what your child wants to say. Encourage them to share their thoughts with you – I can hear some of you saying 'my child/teenager won't tell me anything and they won't listen to me'. It starts when they are toddlers, they soon find out if you are listening to them and sharing your own feelings with them. They are more aware than we give them credit for. You may be yelling at them over some minor issue, then Mary Jones from down the street arrives and you put on a sweet smile and start calling the kids 'darling'! They know you, they can see right through your show. It's time to take down the shutters, time to stop pretending that everything is sweet and lovely and look at how you communicate with your youngsters.

If communication with your child/teenagers was broken at a very early age, if somehow you felt they would inhibit your own wellbeing, your style, they felt they just had to fit in around you – it may be causing great traumas now. But it can be retrieved with some understanding and help; however, it is better and easier if the communication starts right from those first moments of bonding at birth. It doesn't just happen, it takes time and energy. Precious time, when you feel maybe you should be out socializing, working, playing bingo, at the pub or a thousand other things, even going to church, preaching, evangelising or visiting an old lady.

May I say I am not criticisng you, I understand the pressure. I am not against women working, my husband feels I am a much happier person when I do something outside the home. There was a survey taken once on women; they found out that women who went out to work spent more time actively with their children, as if somehow the guilt made them overcompensate. Whether this is a true picture or not, it makes a point. Beware when you think 'I have given up work for my family'. Do you give yourself to them, or are you constantly telling them what a hero you are and how indebted they are to you?

Whatever your situation, start to reach out to love to your children. If this is new to you, keep on, it will become part of you as you practise loving them. Here's an example. When a friend, vicar, priest or acquaintance comes to your door, you may just have done all your housework, painted the kitchen, mended the car, had a hard day at the office or just rushed in from work to prepare the evening meal. When you open the door to your visitor generally you put on a smile, offer them a cup of coffee or tea, or a drink of wine. You spend time, even if it's only a few minutes to show some care. Imagine when the doorbell rang and it was your child or teenager, your reaction might be 'Why didn't you go around the back?' or 'Take your shoes off when you come in, you're always so scruffy when you come home from school', or 'I don't know what people will think of me when they see you so scruffy', or 'Before you get in front of that telly, come and help me, I've been working all day'. We heap on to those we (supposedly) love all our negative attitudes. We do it to our husbands, wives and children. We somehow feel it doesn't matter – we have a right to do it. Listen to yourself, think of the things you say. Do they help love to grow in your family? Do they make your children feel accepted so they would share with you some fears or concerns that they have? Husbands, do you take the attitude 'Well, she's my wife, she should do this or that'. Wives, do you take time to welcome your husband home – you've been busy, but he has been facing the angry world all day, he needs you to reach out to him. It's no good blaming him when he has been unfaithful. Maybe you were so busy with 'things' that you neglected his feelings, his needs to be loved and cared for.

Next time your kids come in from school with dirty feet, instead of saying all the negative things that they already know, say something positive like 'Hi Jimmy, it's nice to see you. Can I get you a drink or something?' Or your husband comes home and he's late. You usually nag him that his supper is ruined and you're not just there to be a slave. Think! It isn't easy to start, when you hear the sound of the car or the door open, pop the kettle on for a nice cup of tea, then go and meet him. Put your arms around him and tell him how nice it is he is home! Let me tell you, these things don't always come naturally, but when you reach out in love it has beautiful repercussions.

In our family relationships we need to give up always wanting our own way. We are constantly bombarded about 'our rights'. If you take on the role of the servant, be gentle and giving, you will find that others will be in turn freed to serve you. Let me assure you, you won't become a doormat but you will encourage others in the family to love.

When we look at the example of Jesus and God the Father, we find God was so willing to give Jesus up to this sinful world. When Jesus came to this world he came as a little baby, helpless, feeding from his mother's breast, toddling around her legs, receiving love and discipline from Joseph. Have you ever thought how you would have reacted in such circumstances? To be given a baby in such unusual circumstances? Somehow humanly we reject the idea, we think that God is not personally interested in our situation. It's OK for some special people but not for me. I want to say to you that God is interested in you. He knows you. He knows the unusual circumstances into which you were born, He understands why you react under certain pressure, He knows why you feel like running away at times, why you feel hard done by, why you feel nobody understands you and if they really knew how you felt they would not want to know you. Just listen, God formed you within the womb of your mother. It says in the Bible, 'He knit me together in my mother's womb'. He knew you before you were born and He knows the situation you have been born into. He knows the stigma. He knows the insecurity, the sadness, the poverty, the problems that wealth brings. He knows your exact situation, and not only does He know but He planned for you to be born into that situation.

Think of this. In the same way that God planned the birth of His Son Jesus into such extraordinary circumstances, He planned your birth. You are not an accident, the very God, the Creator, planned for you to be born. Neither is your child an accident.

As Paul developed, I somehow knew that God must have felt pain when He allowed Jesus to be born into this unusual situation, and yet we see in the Bible it says, 'He spared not His own Son'. It took me a while to come to terms with this because I felt it was rather a cruel thing to accept that a Father who loved could give such pain to his Son. This was carried on in my feelings towards my own children. If God really loved us, why did He allow Paul to suffer so much pain? Why couldn't he have just been the same as other children?

We faced many desperate and dark moments. It was crazy to look any further than the present day. We determined with the three youngsters that we would live every day to the full and not be constantly looking forward to something further on. We knew that God was for us even in the face of these unusual circumstances. Although the situation brought heartache and many tears, we knew God loved us. Meanwhile we constantly fed God's love into our kids, both by serving them and speaking into their lives God's life, His words and His thoughts. Don't get me wrong, I am not saying you must have 'Family Prayers' at mealtimes, or you must have 'Family Altar' once a day. No! . . . what I am saying is that our lives must express the very nature and life of God. We must be consistent with our children, but not necessarily always right. We must express power, through the Spirit of God, into the many and diverse situations that arise within the family unit.

When we think of God, we have some strange pictures, depending on whether our background is Catholic, Protestant, Church of England, Non conformist, Jewish, Greek Orthodox, Muslim or Hindu. Whatever your background, whatever your image of God, I want you to know that the great God – Jehovah who created the universe, the one who sent Jesus, His very own Son, to die for our sins to be forgiven and our sicknesses to be healed – is alive today. He is interested in you, He loves you so much. He knows that you fear Him. In a way He commands respect, praise and worship from us. He is our Creator, He is majestic and powerful. He can speak and the winds will stop, at His word the blind will see, when He speaks the lame will leap for joy. I want you to know that the Spirit of God is moving upon this land, indeed right throughout the whole world. In the Bible it promises that in the last days God will pour out His Spirit upon all flesh, upon male and female, upon adults and children. God wants to be involved in your life, He knows who you are, he knows the difficulties you face, He knows about your job, your mortgage your housing problems, the guilt you feel about what you have done. Nobody else fully understands the intricacies of the situation, but God does. He loves you, and He has chosen you to be His very own person. You may feel rejected by 'The Church' because they didn't help you, they didn't really understand the things with which you needed help. Christians whom you thought would help have let you down. They really only made you feel more condemned. God wants to heal your situation. He won't let you down. His love is so sure even in the face of adverse circumstances.

God sent His very own son Jesus to this earth for you. 'God spared not His own Son'. He allowed him to die on the Cross of Calvery so that you could be free from guilt, free from the things that bind you or control you, so that your sicknesses could be healed, so that the love between parents and children can be renewed and the unhappiness and heartache caused by broken marriages can have new life put into them. I want you to realise that I am not talking about attending church, or not going to the pub, or being a goody-goody. No, I am talking about real life, not just on a Sunday, or when visitors call, but every day. God wants to live right in you. He wants to give you a new start in life, He wants to forgive your sins and cleanse you. You must cry out to Him and ask forgiveness. He is right with you now listening to you. He wants to put His Spirit, the Holy Spirit of God, right within you. Ask Him!

Strange, thinking about sons really. Mary had an unusual task bringing up Jesus, the Son of God. Do you know you have a similar task with your children? Beware that you don't hold onto them too tightly, they are put within your care not to be controlled so much that they just become an extension of yourself, but for you to develop and bring out their own characters. Then at the correct time to allow them or even encourage them to fly from the nest.

I can identify with Mary. When Jesus was twelve he got left behind on the journey and his parents returned looking for him and found him talking to the leaders in the Temple. Parents, what would you have felt like? How would you have reacted? He said to them 'I must be about my Father's business'. I wonder if they thought 'you're an unthoughtful, inconsiderate child.' They could have put an awful lot of pressure on Him to conform, to be like the other children staying close to their parents' side. But no, I believe they realised that God was in control of this little one.

7

Bringing Healing To Others – But What About Paul?

AGAIN IN JUNE 1977, Mr. Norman reviewed Paul's situation. He contacted the school about the level of Paul's achievement – it was very low. He advised on particular learning aids and explained that it was no use looking at reading in isolation. We all needed to look and work at clarity of speech and comprehension to help him to use what he heard in real life experience and to cope with pencil and paper skills. Maybe to encourage him to write a story for a younger child, to help boost his own confidence and self-esteem.

The days and months seemed so long, we really wanted a quick answer to our problem. One day the church family met together to pray for certain aspects of the church life. Andy and I felt so low, we contemplated whether we should actually attend this gathering. Generally people would seek us out to share their problems and to look for encouragement, but that night we felt we had to be honest with this group. Paul was so heavy on our hearts and spirits, he was facing such frustration and heartache. We wished we could bear it for him but we couldn't. Before this point, although people knew there was a problem, they weren't fully aware of the complexities of it. Andy and I wept as we shared with them the heartache. When we prayed for other people they were often healed.

Beautiful miracles took place, people were revitalised, marriages healed, children united with parents, people who had suffered traumas and rejection felt totally accepted and loved. Why didn't God do something for Paul? It was an embarrassing situation. We had to expose our deep feelings to this group of people whom we would normally be counselling or encouraging. We knew their weaknesses and shortcomings, and yet we had to ask them for help. They wept with us. They pleaded with God to do something. Like us, they wanted a miracle. And something did happen. It wasn't quite what we expected. Quite unexpectedly a middle-aged lady spoke, and it was right from God. She said:

'Paul is my chosen son, he is a very special servant of mine. I have chosen him for a special task. I love him. The situation he is in is not a mistake. I have ordained it. I see and know the heartache but it is because of my love that my hand is upon him. I am doing it for my glory. I will constantly be with him. I will never leave him.'

Yes, we heard this but somehow it didn't relieve the problems he faced now. It did bring us some comfort that God was never going to leave him. We explained to Paul what had happened and conveyed to him what God, through prophecy, had said. He accepted it joyfully. He was so confident that, whatever happened in life, God was for him. He wanted to be God's servant, even if it meant pain and isolation. His life has taught us so many things. He is so disciplined and well motivated to work hard at whatever task is before him.

During those years in the early seventies, both Andy and I were becoming more aware of God's anointing on us. I realised that as I looked at people I was aware of situations and difficulties that they were in. I had always been able to listen to problems and empathise with people, but this was different. Thoughts would come into my mind, pictures, words and visions. I would know about a situation that nobody had told me.

I clearly recall a situation with a very pretty twenty-year-old girl. Joan had encountered emotional problems right back through her school life, and on into her teens. She came from a nice home with a very caring mum. Her dad was caring but didn't show his feelings very much. He was quite silent at times. There were some grown-up children from her mum's previous marriage. Joan never felt people wanted her. She would withdraw from many situations. She was a very talented young lady, lovely with young children and very attractive to the opposite sex. She was a Christian but somehow felt that God would reject her if he really knew what she was like. After quite a lot of stress, she spent some time in a psychiatric hospital. She was devastated and the medication seemed to give her a dry throat all the time. Andy and I counselled her for many hours. She had weeks of psychotherapy and group therapy. The psychiatrist tried very hard but couldn't find the answer. It was so sad to see her. Life stretched out in front of her, and yet she was in this awful depressive state.

One particular day Andy and I didn't know what to do with her or for her. We had come to the end of all of our answers. The only thing we could do was pray for her. We had done this many times before. Now we were desperate. We prayed: 'God, we don't know the answer but we need a miracle' and, as we held this girl, who was so sad, something happened. A thought came into my mind, 'pray for her birth'. I couldn't understand it but felt it was worth a try. I spoke out aloud. 'God, you created this child, you formed her within her mother's womb. Right inside that darkness you knew Joan. You were forming her little body because you wanted her to be born.' As I prayed, grief overtook me, I felt such anguish. This little baby was withdrawing back into the womb. She didn't want to be born. I do not know how to express it fully but it was as if we were in the Delivery Room again. This baby kept wanting to climb back into the womb and curl up. Somehow Andy, Joan and I were all involved in this scene. I felt the need to verbalise the situation and said, 'Joan, God has formed your body, you are not an accident or mistake. You might have been an accident as far as your parents were concerned, but God has formed you and chosen you. You can safely come out of the womb knowing that God is planning and waiting for you.' We just lingered and waited to see what God would do. After about five minutes, Joan, who was all curled up like a little ball, began to straighten up. I asked: 'What is happening Joan?'. She said: 'I'm coming out and Jesus is waiting at the end of the table for me.' We waited, her face was peaceful although tearful. She shouted: 'He's reaching out his hands to pick me up.' Again we waited, then Andy asked, 'Joan, what's happening now?' She replied: 'He's holding me. He's cuddling me. He really wants me. He's been waiting for me all this time.' Somehow her emotions were reborn. Later we discovered that she was born at a hard time. She wasn't really planned for by her parents, although they loved her when she arrived. Even within the womb she felt the panic, the rejection. But through the Holy Spirit God had healed the rejection that day.

Of course, that was not the end. She continued to need to be shown love and acceptance. She had ups and downs and needed to be constantly assured that we loved her, and that she was a beautiful person. Since then she has blossomed like a rose. She holds a very responsible job and has been such an encouragement and strength to others. Many have been touched by her gentleness.

Let me tell you about a young man whom God touched. David is a man but has suffered so much heartache and rejection. He was so fearful of anyone in authority and so sad and dejected. When we first met him he was eighteen years old, bright, but not fulfilling his potential. He was such a gentle chap but always looked sad. A friend from school had invited him to church where he had heard that God loved him and that he was very special to God, chosen and precious. When God looked on him, He delighted in him. David had been born overseas when his dad was working abroad. The family returned to England just as he was due to start school. He was from a large family that suffered from many marriage problems. His parents continued living in the same house but led independent lives. The children fended for themselves. David was doing his own washing, buying and cooking his own food from the age of fourteen. If he spoke to his mum, his dad was upset. If he spoke to his dad, his mum would get mad. She would attack him physically at times. He had vivid memories of these occasions.

I suppose because of my maternal instincts, I wanted to help him. He was like a little lost boy. God not only wanted to touch his emotions, He wanted him to experience love in the areas of deprivation. It struck me so much one Sunday morning when the church met together. Here was David going home to a can of baked beans, that wasn't so bad, but he would have to eat them all on his own. Most people would be going home to have a delicious three-course meal served with love. God began to show us all that we needed to be looking and doing something about each other's needs. David eventually moved in and lived with one of the families and he blossomed during this time.

We had chatted occasionally on a one-to-one basis about his difficulties. We knew that God wanted to expose some of these areas of pain and heal them. I explained to him how it was good to have a male involved in the counselling, as well as myself, as this brings a security and covering against the evil powers that bind people's lives. We had tried to make a time convenient to Andy, David and myself when we could spend some time together, and also a convenient venue. Often when a person has been deeply hurt or is bound, he will express it in deep sobs, shouts or screams. So we avoid using our home for deep counselling sessions. We were so busy and time was so short, and David was getting more desperate.

It was coming up to the holidays, when we were going away as a church family to a Bible Week. This seemed to be the answer, so we booked the Tuesday afternoon to spend with David. The children would have gone swimming with the group and we would be free. Andy had an elders' meeting which should have finished much earlier, but these sometimes tend to go on! I could see that David was really desperate. I knew that God was with me but I also needed a man. I looked around our camp site and spotted a young man looking rather miserable! He was a bit down in the dumps because of some pressures on his life. I spoke to him: 'Brett, I know you feel miserable but here is your brother who is far worse off than you are. Are you prepared to minister to his needs with me? I know you are weak but it is God's strength.' To my amazement he rose to the challenge, stood up, put his arm around David and off we went to find a suitable spot to talk and pray. It was halfway up the deserted grandstand overlooking the camp site. We chatted for about fifteen minutes about David's life and the past. I asked him to explain to Brett what he had shared with me. As David did this, he began to sob. We encouraged him to carry on even though it hurt. He talked about his mum attacking him with a broom and, as he spoke, he was writhing with pain, his whole body convulsing. I encouraged Brett just to hold him firmly. He needed to express this deep anguish which he had felt for so many years. As he talked on about different incidents, his body vibrated with deep sobs. It was as if God had removed the stopper that had been bottling up all these hurts for so many years. Brett and I just sat and held him as he experienced these bitter pains. Then, as he began to calm a little, we prayed that these empty spaces would now be filled with God's love and power and with the Holy Spirit. He was so overwhelmed that God loved him and that he was for him and not against him. What happened that day we do not know in technical terms. What we do know is that his life was like a flower unfolding, which had been stunted but God has spoken life into it. When we walked back into our part of the camp site, Brett was practically having to hold David up. He was like a drunken man. For God had performed an operation, He had opened up parts in David's life that no psychotherapy could reach. We knew that in the days and weeks to come he would need lots of tender loving care.

Over the next weeks he grew emotionally and the change in him was apparent. He belonged and he was loved. God is very gentle, He wants to remove our fears and hurts. Sometimes they are so much part of our personality that to remove them without providing an alternative is dangerous. He gently waits for the best moment. He generally doesn't remove all the hurts in one go, which is what happened with David. About eight weeks after this experience, he approached me again and asked if we could meet, as he knew there was something else inside him that God was touching. These released emotions kept welling up inside him. He said it was really urgent, so we arranged to meet one Sunday evening in the upstairs lounge of our local Baptist Church after the Sunday evening service. I asked Colin, who was then the Youth Leader, to join us. We didn't have to do any probing or prompting, we just said, 'God, David has a great big pain. We want you to touch and heal it.' Colin prayed over him and together we proclaimed God's power over David's life. I explained to Colin what I anticipated might happen and that he might need to hold David so that he didn't hurt himself. It was good that we had prepared ourselves, for this poor kid was so overcome with the deepest heartache. He writhed on the floor in pain and needed to be held like a baby. We took it in turns to pray for him and observe him. It was hard work. We were totally exhausted. I was so sure that God had this all under control, but we needed extra human help. I went down into the church to see if Andy or one of the other elders were there but they couldn't be found. There was only one gentleman there, Graham Coles, the Administrator. I had never counselled with Graham before and wondered how he would cope with this boy who was so distressed. I had always thought of Graham as the 'typical English gentleman' but God knew best. I said 'Graham, we desperately need the help of a strong man with David.' He was just the father figure that David needed, it was amazing. By this time things had calmed down a little bit, this nineteen year old, who was five feet nine inches tall, needed to be held like a baby and Colin and I were exhausted. But Graham picked him up and cradled him for the next forty-five minutes. Again we are unaware of the exact detail of what took place in his body, mind, emotions and spirit. We just knew it was a mighty undoing of the hurts he had experienced over the years. Then the joy and peace came and David lay in Graham's arms helpless but so peaceful. God had performed a mighty healing in his life. To see this young man now brings tears of joy to my eyes. We really love him and he is being used mightily by God in the leading of worship and reaching out to other young people. 'Thank you Lord, you are so gracious and your kindness is from generation to generation.'

On another occasion a young mum came to me very distraught. She had just given birth to her first baby and he was beautiful. I know that the normal mother instinct is not to want to leave her baby. Andy always joked with me when our children were babies. He said I was like a little dog who had had puppies. I couldn't even walk around the block without wanting to run back to see if they were all right. But this lassie was overcome with fear. She was grief-stricken even if her husband was with the child, which was not a normal maternal instinct. It was real fear. Another mum and

I met together to pray for Kathy. We chatted and then began to pray. As we did this Kathy began to sob, so we allowed her to carry on. After about ten minutes, I asked 'What has happened?'. She said, 'I feel as if I am a baby and I'm being left on my own again. It's ages and ages and nobody has been to see me.' These memories continued to come and we just held her and assured her that Jesus was always with her. He was never going to leave her. After a few moments she began to move. I asked 'What is happening, Kathy?' She said, 'Jesus has picked me up and is holding me. He is holding me! He hasn't left me!' A beautiful rest and peace came over her countenance. After this experience, she still very much loved her baby but was able to leave him for periods without being totally distraught.

One Sunday a new gentleman came into the church. It was quite common to see new people coming in. As he sat down God said to me 'He has a sexual problem in his family.' I had never even talked to the man. I had never seen him before. What did I do with this information? I didn't feel I should blurt it out in the middle of the meeting. Later on I explained to one of the elders what had happened. He chatted to him and discovered that this was so. It was quite a complex situation. God had shown this early on so that in the years to come we would be able to help to bring him into a full release.

It was in the context of healings like these that we were struggling with our our own son's problems. At times we were so puzzled and low and wondering why the God who loved us appeared unaware of our cries. Then, at other times, we felt encouraged and our hopes rose again. One of these slight encouragements came at the end of the Summer Term 1977, when Paul was ten. His report that July read:–

Conduct: Good
Attitude: Good
Special qualities: He is very inventive

Summary: Paul has worked very hard and with interest.

He joins in well with class discussions and has a good general knowledge. He is doing all he can to overcome his difficulties and he deserves to succeed.

Class teacher: Mrs A. Thomas
Headteacher: Mr. B. J. Vincent

The very next month, August 1977, Mr. Norman again met Paul and made an assessment of his development. He reported as follows to Mr. Vincent:

Mr. B. J. Vincent, 9th August 1977
Butler's Court Middle School,
Beaconsfield,
Bucks.

Dear Mr. Vincent,

re: Paul Croall – 4.4.67

As arranged at the recent case conference in school I have seen Paul and carried out an assessment of his reading and spelling skills. The results gained were as follows:

Holborn Reading Scale – reading age 8 years
Daniels and Diack Reading Test – reading age 8 years 6 months
Daniels and Diack Spelling Test – spelling age 8 years 1 month

As usual, Paul presented in a chatty, friendly and open manner, appearing relaxed and at ease from the outset of the session. His flow of language has improved but it still somewhat halting and at times he has to search for the right word. I found his speech a little difficult to understand at times, partly because of his accent, and partly because of his immaturities of articulation. He has particular difficulty with the 'r' sounds. This will not have helped him to gain reading in the past. His conversation ranged over many different and interesting topics and on occasions he used this as a way to avoid the reading test.

I saw Paul about a year ago and in that time he has made approximately one year's progress. Although his reading still lacks fluency his word attack skills have improved and he is better able to make use of context cues. Mrs. Dell has continued with the Cloze exercises as suggested earlier and I feel that these would still pay dividends. Paul himself now feels more confident in his reading, is aware of the progress being made, and tells me that he reads both for pleasure and information. His father later told me that he uses his reading skills extensively in his hobby of stamp collecting. I feel that a continuing programme of work to extend his visual vocabulary, improve his fluency of reading, and build up his confidence in his own skills is indicated. He has now acquired the basic phonic attack skills. Emphasis must be placed on finding reading material which is stimulating, relevant and within his capability.

Progress has also been made on the spelling side. Paul's writing continues to be poorly formed, large and untidy and I will discuss the possibility of some specific help in this area with the class teacher. His spelling is now at about the eight to eight-and-a-half year level and he copes well on phonically regular words. He has more difficulty with the irregular words where he cannot apply his phonic skills. To help him here I would suggest either the memory trace approach or Fernald's multi sensory method. I will discuss both of these with Mrs. Dell next term.

It would seem that Mr. Croall is happy with the progress that Paul is making and feels that everything is being done in his child's best interests. It has been agreed that a further review of Paul's progress will be made shortly after Christmas.

Yours sincerely,
P. F. Norman
Senior Educational Psychologist

For Paul to have progressed so well really encouraged us. It was minimal compared to other children but it was a move forward.

Then September arrived, Paul was in a new class with a new teacher. His teacher's initial remarks were 'His English is weak/poor and work very untidy. Maths is better and he is not unintelligent.'

By the time March 1978 arrived Paul was experiencing great difficulty with his teacher. He was a bright child, we always knew this, and this is what caused so much frustration to him. He was always good at maths although sometimes he would reverse his figures. One day I picked him up from school, he looked so sad walking up to the car, he was on his own – he was usually on his own, this made me sad as well. As we drove home I asked 'What happened today, Paul?' With such pain he said to me 'Why do they keep me in the bottom maths set, I know what they are doing in the other group and I can do it.' Because his written presentation was very poor, he was excluded from what he could do well. Andy and I visited the school and when they realised this they moved him into the other group and he did excellently!

We worked very hard at helping our children, Paul, Barry and Ruth, to look at themselves positively. They probably wouldn't ever be the brightest in school, but we wanted them to be acceptable as themselves. In fact, we want each of them to be themselves, although they are so different to each other.

As parents, we had become aware of the need to praise success and never to reprimand incorrect responses. One problem with this was what we should do about those few teachers who didn't have much understanding of Paul's difficulty? Did we expose him to Cub Scouts, First Aid etc.? I really wanted to protect him from the harshness of some people's attitudes, but I found I had to encourage him to do things outside the home and teach him about people and their hang-ups.

When you encounter a handicapped child with blindness, walking difficulty or a missing or deformed limb, your hearts go out to them. We can see the handicap, it is awful, but we are aware of it. The sad thing is when you meet a deaf child it is so easy to misunderstand and think they are being rude. It is hard to understand deafness, it brings with it other problems for the person, as they cannot communicate very easily because they cannot speak. In my work in Health Education I used to visit a deaf school once a month. It was hearbreaking but also very rewarding. My aim was to teach these children how to look after their teeth. They looked very normal, but to communicate was very difficult. I always admired the way the staff managed to understand these children and make the children understand them.

Dyslexia brings with it similar difficulties. The child looks as if everything is fine. They are faced with anger because teachers feel they are not trying. When they really try hard, their work is so untidy that it gets big red crosses through it. The very effort of trying to read is so tiring. I remember going through very early learning books with Paul at nine and ten years old, and eventually I would think he was reading, but in fact he was reciting it. He had learnt the whole book by heart! Some of the problems with this handicap are:
Confusion of letters – e.g. d b; u n.

Reversal of letters – e.g. was-saw; dog-god.
Small word confusion – e.g. of, for, from.
Difficulty in pronouncing – merains-remains; uminimous-unanimous.
Mispronouncing some words – renember, rememory.
Shortening words – rember-remember.
Fusion of letters.
Badly formed letters.
Confusion between right and left.
Difficulty in sequencing – alphabet; months of the year.
Difficulty in learning tables.
Difficulty in telling time.
Late in things like tying shoe laces.
Left-handedness of mixed laterality.
These are sometimes difficult to diagnose because children vary in their development. Paul first started holding his pencil with his left hand and later switched over to his right hand.

Barry and Ruth had never laughed at Paul, his difficulty was an open subject, we didn't feel it was something to be ashamed of, they were all individual people. Both Ruth and Barry were very quick at reading and writing and at many other things. My heart used to break sometimes when I would see Ruth, so young, sitting reading to Paul. Or Barry, reading every word that came on the TV programme that Paul wanted to watch. Paul gained a lot of his understanding from watching TV documentaries with either Barry or Ruth reading out loud the necessary parts. He got so frustrated if his train of thought was broken.

Around this time we bought Paul a calculator, because we wanted to do anything that would help him. He was so pleased and promptly added up the ages of all the family Then he came to me so confused saying, 'Mum, this can't be right, they must come to more than 19.' I checked the reading on the calculator, it was 91. This will help you understand the confusion. Another day, coming up to Christmas, Paul claimed a part of a kitchen cupboard to store his goodies in. He put a big notice on it:

TUO PEEK ETAVIRP

It was totally reversed, but when we gently questioned him about it he didn't realise it was the wrong way around.

On another occasion we had a family day out to Canterbury Cathedral. The kiddies were so excited and the sun was shining As we piled into the car we had to watch our vunerable conflict moments and try to avoid or distract. We realised that, as we started off on a journey and, as we were about to arrive at our destination, were the times there was most likely to be a fight in the back of the car. All went well, the kids were very happy with each other and life in general. We wandered around this beautiful building, looked at all the interesting parts then wandered through the grounds. There were little notices pointing to places of interest. Barry was so quick, he would only be eight years old, Ruth Six and Paul ten. Andy and I were walking hand in hand and the children running in front and behind, suddenly Barry and Ruth disappeared up this lovely, exciting looking path, Paul just walked silently by us. Andy asked 'Paul, why didn't you go with Barry and Ruth?' Paul replied, 'Barry told me the notice said it was only for children under ten years old.' In fact the notice only said 'Public Conveniences' so hastily Paul followed. That is only a little example of this handicap. Barry was pulling Paul's leg! I must say we took Barry aside and had a little chat in his ear! We explained to him the meaning of 'taking advantage'.

8

Assessing Our Priorities

AT THIS STAGE in our lives, when Paul was around ten years old, we were really struggling. Every day we had to give time to try and help him to read and write – it was so disheartening. It was so difficult to balance his learning/language difficulty with the need for him to be a happy individual in other areas of life. We had to weigh every situation. Should he watch his favourite TV programme if this was the only time we could fit in reading? Should we carry on trying to help him on holiday? If he lost the continuity it would be worse for him when he returned to school after the holiday. It was so difficult to come to the right decision. We always talk to our kids if we don't know the answer, or if we are deciding something concerning them, like time-keeping. It is amazing if you let them come to a decision with you, rather than being told 'You are going to do this.'

This particular time we were so tired and frustrated, we wanted the best for the family. We knew that Paul desperately needed extra help at home. Andy and I could help him to a certain extent, but we were so emotionally involved it was difficult sometimes. We also wanted to avoid any jealousy from Barry and Ruth. Our big problem was that we just couldn't afford to get a private teacher who specialized in this area of learning. Lessons would cost at least £7 an hour.

For many months past we had been counselling a young lady called Wendy. She was a lovely girl but got so depressed at times, she had tried to take her own life on many an occasion. She had gone through the trauma of a divorce and her baby dying. Strangely enough she was a teacher but had not taught for a long time because of her depression. She was constantly at our home pouring out her troubles. Many emotions in her life had been touched and healed.

This particular week we were struggling so hard with Paul's situation. He was nearly eleven years old and still could hardly read or write. Andy had been trying to give him half an hour a night to help him but with his work, church, home and the other two children it was very difficult. We came to the end of ourselves (I'm crying again as I recall the pain of this time). We were faced with Paul's secondary education – what can we do? We looked at all possibilities. Boarding school? Private school? State school? Boarding school we thought might have good academic facilities going for it, but no, we felt that to be involved in family life was far more important. Private school, no chance – we just would not be able to afford it. So our only choice was to stay in the State School System.

Andy is usually so patient with people, especially with people who may be suffering from depression or mental pressure. But this day I was amazed at his reaction. I was in the lounge with Barry and Ruth, Andy was in our upstairs office with Paul, trying to help. The doorbell rang, I opened it, and there was Wendy, depressed, crying and complaining. I would not allow her into the lounge because of the children, so I was talking to her in the dining room, right underneath the office. The conversation went like this, 'How did you get in this state, Wendy?' reply, 'Because nobody cares about me, and nobody spends time with me.' I could hardly believe my ears – we had spent hours and hours with this lassie. Andy heard the commotion and came downstairs and he received the same comments. He was so furious, he said, 'Wendy, I spend all these hours counselling you, and I've an eleven year old son upstairs who can't read or write, and you're a teacher. You could be helping him, instead you come here moaning and wasting my time so that I can't help him.' Wow! I was so amazed at Andy's reaction, the atmosphere was really charged. Andy went back up to Paul and I had a cup of coffee with Wendy. She went home not knowing quite what had hit her. The next evening she arrived with her books under her arm and for the next year spent two or three nights a week working with Paul. She was a fantastic teacher and so patient with him. This was the beginning of Paul really making any sense of letters and figures, and the beginning of Wendy coming to terms with herself and reaching out to others. They had an interesting relationship. Paul would sometimes ask me to give Wendy someone else to think about because she was thinking about herself too much. On a number of occasions I have seen Paul put his arm around her and pray for her. He was only a child but this handicap had given him so much insight into other people's handicaps, whether they were visible or not visible. How we all need to learn not to despise a handicap, whether it is in ourselves, our child, or another person. Each person is precious and has something to give to others. We need constantly to seek to bring out the best in other people, especially in our children.

In our own family we knew we couldn't hide from heartache and pain. We either had to pretend that there were no problems, or look them in the eye in a very realistic way and find ways that would best take us through them. For example: when Paul was eleven years of age we were faced with a choice of holidays. Some of the children we knew were going on a 'Warrior Camp', and it gives me a horrible sinking feeling in my stomach as I recall the pain of that year. Paul was not keen to go, he was so different to other kids. Remember, he couldn't even read what it said on the Information Sheet about the holiday. We didn't want to expose him in order to hurt him, but we realised if we didn't encourage him to go on this camp he again would be different. He would be a loner, not relating to others even on the things he could do.

It was quite a physical kind of camp with organised games and competitions. When we talked with Paul about it I remembered the agony of myself at school. When there was competition, I hated it, and it really hurt to think of Paul in this situation. I wanted to say, 'Paul, never mind, you just stay at home with me and I will take you out each day.' Andy was so aware of my feelings and so graciously and strongly acknowledged them in Paul's presence, but then said 'Paul, you have a difficulty, sometimes on this holiday you will feel like running away but, son, we love you, you are a lovely lad, we love you just as you are. We want you to look this problem in the eye and work at it.' Please understand, it wasn't easy to expose Paul to this situation. We knew they would do ball games which he hated because he couldn't co-ordinate properly at all. He enjoyed swimming which was one of the main activities, but he swam differently to the others and it had taken a long, long time to help him learn to swim. Orienteering was another major activity of the camp and he enjoyed this, although it caused him problems.

The day he went he was excited but also apprehensive. Paul knew it took him ten times as long as the other children to read a notice board – and some camps are full of notices! During the week another difficulty cropped up when the camp staff organised Bible competitions with the children when they had to write down the answers to questions. This was, of course, impossible for Paul, so although he knew the answers he was unable ever to win.

Prior to committing Paul to going on this camp, Andy and I had talked to the camp leaders to explain the problem. We didn't want to expose Paul to something that was going to be totally negative. We made them aware of the difficulty and advised them on no account to ask Paul to read out aloud.

The leader's wife, Joyce Scott, has suffered ill-health herself during the years and she became very special to Paul. I don't think she has realised how much her understanding meant to Paul and to us. Writing down the answers for the competition was in full swing with a lovely, new Bible as the prize for the children who completed the questions. Poor Paul, he had no chance, he knew the answers but it took him so long even to write his name, and even that was difficult to understand. But Joyce Scott took time to hear the answers from him orally, and then encouraged him to write the answers down at home in his own time. It wouldn't matter how long it took him, she kept tabs on him. He didn't have the joy of receiving his Bible with the other children at camp, but two months later he handed in his completed work, some of it illegible, but he received his Bible. He was so delighted, he might have just been given £10,000!

This is a sample of his writing then. He sent us this postcard from that camp:

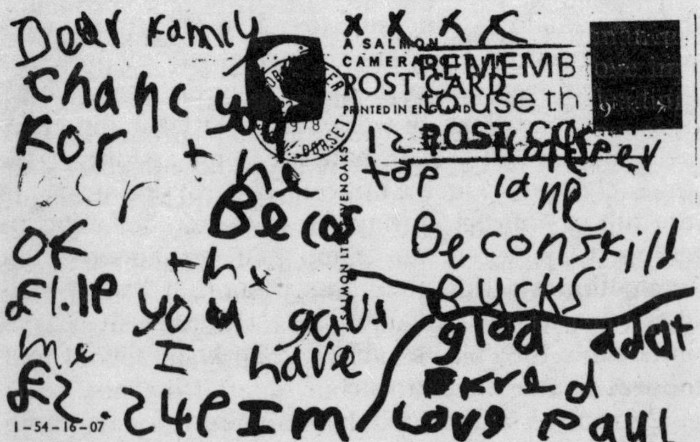

Somehow he had started to come to terms with his handicap. In school he had been kept in at playtime to catch up on his work and he had missed his favourite lessons to have more time to learn to read and write, he really couldn't win. We had tried very hard to build up his self-esteem and at last something seemed to be happening.

On 30th March 1978, Mr. Norman reveiwed again, when Paul was eleven years old. He sent a letter to the headmaster, saying that Paul's flow of language was still poor, and he had difficulty with sound sequencing in words, also his recall of facts was limited. He had a reading age of eight years six months, but a comprehension age of twelve years two months. At this interview we chatted about Paul's secondary education. He didn't have a chance of passing the 12+ test to be selected for Grammar School. In Buckinghamshire we still have Selective Education, this means that at the age of twelve plus the child has to sit an examination which will assess his ability for Grammar School or Secondary School. We knew there was no possibility of Paul gaining a place in a Grammar School, he just wouldn't cope. He would find it very, very difficult to cope in a Secondary School.

Three miles from our home there was a Secondary School which had a Dyslexia Unit. This seemed to be the answer, the only problem was that to secure a place in this specialist resource centre Paul needed to go through the specialist educational process. This involved reports being written on his difficulties by staff at his present school, and Dr. Burne, and Mr. Norman, the school psychologist. But because we were not in the catchment area for the school, Paul had to be referred to the Senior Clinical Medical Officer for schools when he was coming up to twelve years old.

At one point we considered a private school and looked at the possibilities but, apart from not being able to afford such a school, we felt that, for Paul, the security of a loving home and family were far more important to his 'whole person' development than to send him off to a boarding school that specialised with children with a specific learning/language problem. We looked at every conceivable possibility. Then, just three miles away from our home, we heard of this State Secondary School with a Dyslexic Unit, called Pembroke School, at Flackwell Heath. Andy telephoned the headteacher and arranged for us to have a look around. We liked what we saw and Paul felt he could be happy there. So, with the help of Mr. Norman, the psychologist, we set the wheels in motion to get Paul to this school and eventually it was arranged for him to start there in September 1979. Both Mr. Norman and the Headteacher from the Unit thought it would be helpful for Paul to attend one afternoon a week prior to actually starting at the school. We all felt Paul would be more relaxed and would learn their teaching methods more easily in the September. So, from January 1979 until the end of term in July, I transported Paul to Pembroke School once a week. It was well worth the effort, for, when September came, Paul was raring to go.

We will always be gratefull to Mr. Norman for the many hours he spent helping Paul and ourselves during those years. As the big transition to Secondary School came nearer and we hoped for a place at Pembroke School, Mr. Norman's assessment continued. In January that year he wrote: 'In particular, he still experiences great difficulty in eye/hand manipulation and pencil control tasks and on the coding sub-test gained an extremely poor score, reflecting the difficulty he will have in recording information speedily and tidily. He still has difficulty in coping with sequencing tasks, e.g. days of the week, months of the year, but his general knowledge score on this occasion was far superior to when I saw him two and a half years ago. His visual perceptual skills have improved considerably and he has developed excellent visual analysis and integration skills.' The coding sub-test is a test of eye and hand co-ordination and visual matching skills. Also during these months, Mr. Norman kindly spoke to

Wendy Caine who was helping Paul at home and advised her on the correct methods of teaching to use in Paul's situation.

But Paul had still a long, long way to go to catch up with children without learning/language problems. This is a sample of Paul's handwriting in the last year of his middle school, when he was twelve years old:

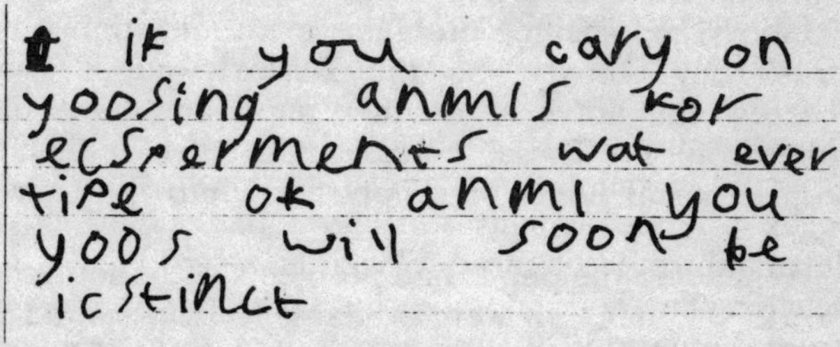

Interpretation: 'If you carry on using animals for experiments, whatever type of animals you use will soon be extinct.'

Paul's new school was an ordinary secondary school but had attached to it a specialist unit, then called 'The Dyslexia Unit'. Recently its name has been changed to 'Department for Pupils with Specific Learning Difficulties'. It was a terrapin building in the grounds of the school, but it serves the whole of South Bucks and so places are very limited and the staff are very stretched. When Paul started there they explained to us that the staff/pupil ratio should ideally be one teacher to three pupils, but since more light has been thrown on the subject of learning difficulties, the pressure for places at the unit has increased. At the Pembroke School the Dyslexic pupils followed a normal secondary education with support. They would have their English lessons in the unit. About 70 per cent of the Dyslexic pupils also have numeracy problems affecting computational skills. These pupils also had their maths lessons in the unit. Pupils not displaying a weakness in mathematical skills followed normal maths lessons in the main school. Paul was one of these Dyslexic pupils who received extra help and support with their main school work in areas of difficulty such as copying from the blackboard and dictation. Since the pupils were referred because of literacy problems, their weakness in reading and their visual sequential memory difficulties made copying very difficult. Auditory confusion, a week auditory memory and spelling problems made dictation a very frustrating activity. So the Dyslexic pupils would borrow the notes of another pupil and have them photocopied. These notes could then either be copied up at home or simply fixed into the exercise books.

Whenever the pupils had problems with their school work, the unit staff were available to help and advise.

The teacher-in-charge of the unit explained the situation within the school to us. She said the Headteacher, Mr. Jones, gave full support to the work of the unit and many of the main school staff were very understanding and gave a lot of assistance to the dyslexic pupils in their teaching groups. But there were some teachers who did not make any allowances for the pupils' learning difficulties, or familiarise themselves with teaching techniques that would have helped the Dyslexic pupils and would have benefited all the other pupils as well. Simple changes in teaching methods and the structuring of work make it possible to include and help pupils with special needs within normal school lessons.

We had always talked to Paul about teachers' attitudes and that they could be negative or ignorant of his difficulty, but it still hurt him if he came up against such an attitude. We wanted him to respect his teachers but we were also aware of some of their hang-ups.

Paul started full-time at Pembroke School in September 1979 when he was twelve. Here is a sample of his work during his first term:

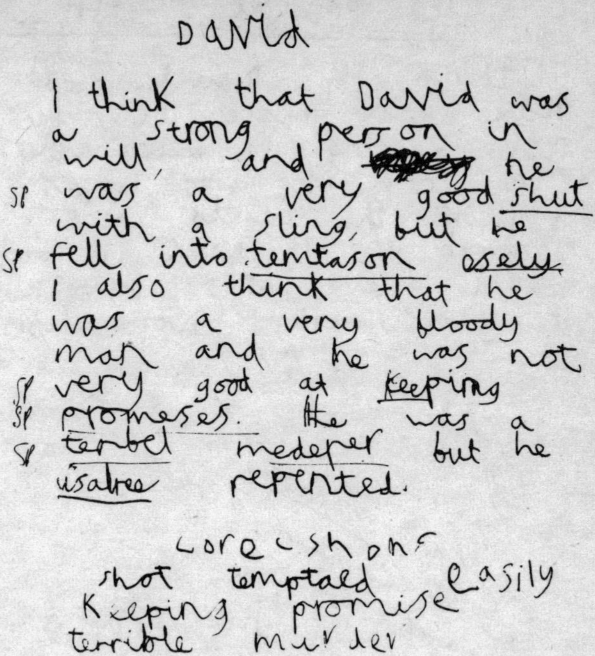
DaVid

I think that DaVid was a strong person in will, and he was a very good shut with a sling, but he fell into temtason esely. I also think that he was a very bloody man and he was not very good at keeping promeses. He was a terbel mederer but he usalree repented.

corecshons

shot temptaed easily
Keeping promise
terrible murder

Even his spelling of 'corrections' was phonetically correct. In fact, most of his words were spelt phonetically correct. He really did try hard because he wanted to succeed. Then on October 12th he brought home his books and we tended to look through his work in the evening because he needed constant help. We were so dismayed when reading the negative comments from one of the teachers, but fortunately I don't think Paul could read his writing. Andy and I were furious! Here was a teacher threatening to punish Paul if he didn't improve. The poor kid, it took him so long to actually write a paragraph like this:

St. Briavels 12th Oct

I think St. Briavels could have been made beter by not haveing so much walking. Also if it was longer. I thort the casels were sooperb so I thenk it ~~wood~~ would have been beter if there were more classes.

Totally unsatisfactory. If there is no improvement in neatness at least by Christmas I shall punish you. J. J. H 10/79.

Once more a visit to the school was necessary.

We discovered with all our children they thrive on praise and positive input into their lives! I remember with deep pain the times we have had to say to Paul, Barry and Ruth that they will come up against things in other people that hurt them. The problem is when these people are in authority – how we need to guard our youngsters and teach them better standards. They have to live in this unjust and unfair society, but we need to help them to know what is right, not to be cheeky but to be aware of other people's attitudes.

9

Preparing For Future Employment

RIGHT FROM EARLY ON in life, Paul's ambition was to be an inventor or manager. Through his early life he wasn't too sure what he would invent or who he would manage. He has always been a good organiser. We sat down one day on holiday to try to trace why we always had disagreement on how to tackle a simple decision. Easy! We realised that in the Croall family we had five very good organisers, each having a very good way of doing things but each quite different! We had encouraged the children to have free expression of their thoughts and ideas, so we had to handle decisions together. For example, on holiday, where shall we go today? What shall we eat? What shall we do? We found it was best to delegate one person to choose and we would all follow – even though we all had our own ideas. Andy would have the final word if any conflict arose. It is a very useful exercise because it not only allows children to develop leadership skills, but also to follow someone else's decision, even if they have a different way of doing it.

As I am writing this, Andy and I are holidaying in Portugal, in the Algarve. We have borrowed a lovely villa with a flat roof to sunbathe on. It is the first time we have left our teenagers for two weeks, although we have been away for a weekend without them. Something interesting happened this morning. I was soaking in the bath and Andy was on the roof. He shouted down the chimney to me saying that it had actually rained in the night and the two long cushions we lie on to sunbathe had got wet. He said 'I've put them across the top of the walls to dry'. I immediately responded 'If you hang them on the line they will dry very quickly'. He roared with laughter and retorted 'I'm glad Paul, Barry and Ruth aren't with us, or there would be three other ways to do it!' I graciously bowed to his decision. When I took a cup of coffee up on the roof three quarters of an hour later they were completely dry.

Paul was always industrious and we looked for ways to help him. We didn't know what his prospects of employment would be. We knew he would do something, he wasn't the type to let the world go by, but even a simple task like coping with a paper round caused him problems.

I remember him coming home to me when he was nearing his twelfth birthday. He had been to see Mrs. Butler in the Post Office to ask if he could do a paper round. He explained to her about his reading difficulty. She was a kind lady and telephoned me to ask what I thought. She would help him sort his papers into the right order and mark them clearly. He wanted to face the challenge, so we encouraged him. On his twelfth birthday he was up at 6 am starting on his paper round and he continued with this for about eight months, he was so conscientious. One day he said to me, 'Mum, I think I am getting too tired at school through getting up early and delivering papers. Is it all right if I tell Mrs. Butler I want to leave?' Of course it was alright, we were glad he had faced the challenge and then decided himself that it was too much at that particular time.

He was very enterprising. When we had the pony he thought he might be able to earn some money by selling manure. There were six horses in the field at this time, so the prospects were good. As Andy and Paul were contemplating this new adventure on their way home from the field, Paul said the first thing he needed to get started was some paper sacks. They were walking along the road and Andy said to Paul 'God knows we need them'. At that moment a wastepaper lorry going to Taplow drove past and an amount of waste blew off the top in a gust of wind, scattering over the hundred yards ahead of them. With hilarity, Andy and Paul quickly picked up ten bags that had been deposited and ran home with sheer delight. His business was on the way. Andy was his first customer. He also delivered to the local old people and enjoyed chatting to them, as they did to him.

Paul thought very much about his future life and his career. He contemplated pottery at one point in his life. From a young child we had encouraged him to go to pottery classes on a Saturday morning. We felt it was something he could enjoy and help him to relax without having to read or write. Eventually he took pottery 'O' Level and gained a good pass. He has made some lovely pieces which sit proudly on our shelves at home but he explained to Andy when he was about twelve years old, 'I enjoy pottery, but I don't think I am good enough to make enough money as a career.' But the prospect was in the back of his mind.

Paul, Barry and Ruth have always been enterprising. Over the years they accumulated so many toys and bits and pieces. We constantly gave things away but they held on to their most treasured possessions. These included an old TV Paul had bought from a jumble sale, and an old record player Barry had bought. Ruth had lots of clothes and toys she had collected. And one day they got together and decided it would be a good idea to have a sale in the front garden. Barry and Ruth prepared the notices while Paul got the tables ready. It was really quite exciting! A fantastic way to get to know the people in the neighbourhood. I helped a little by giving them some clothes, bags and bric-a-brac.

They each had their own table and attracted a lot of custom. It was interesting because they took the initiative to let things go. Had Andy or I suggested the idea to them there would have been an uproar. So very early on in Paul's life he had an eye to business. He would work hard at whatever was his objective at any given time.

During these early years we had contemplated whether we would need to help Paul to be self-employed. Whether he would have difficulty in gaining employment in a firm or other business. We talked with him about all the prospects.

Paul was showing a growing interest in computers, but computers are expensive items. It is not only the computer but the TV and the tape recorder, the disc, and then the printer. Then follow the tapes, discs, manuals, and paper for printing. It is an expensive pastime.

We looked at all this when Paul showed interest in a Sinclair Computer we had borrowed from a friend. He was completely taken by it. Andy said to me, 'Dot, we really must consider a computer for Paul, it could be an investment for his future life'. I knew this was so true but I also knew that our finances were so stretched. Some of these seemingly simple issues of life become so complex when there is a lack of finance. My heart used to ache at times. In the areas where we lived, the kids seemed to get anything they wanted, money was no object. Yet here was Paul whose future career could depend on this, and we couldn't afford it.

So for Paul's Christmas present during his first year in the secondary school we decided, one way or another, we had to afford a small computer. His first computer was a Sinclair – he spent hours working on it. Not playing games, though he did sometimes, but finding out how it worked, what it did, what it couldn't do and designing new programmes. Very soon he had exhausted the memory and we bought him a power pack. He struggled with his old tape recorder, often he would lose his work by transferring it from the computer to the tape. But he wouldn't give up, he would start all over again.

He was getting very involved in computing. With it he was not in competition with people. Somehow the machine would self-correct him and he responded to this. He spent hours in his room. He could make this little machine do anything. Also the machine made his writing clearer and easier to understand. As Roger Carter, Paul's teacher, said 'To communicate with a machine is a good substitute, especially to somebody who has had a difficulty communicating.' Paul exhibited some of his designs at a Home Computer User's Exhibition at Ruislip Library. He was very confident in setting up his stall and attracting custom. Ruth helped Paul by designing a poster to display on his stall and Barry made 'answer slips' for customers to fill in. He sold some of his software that day and was very pleased. So were we all! Eventually he couldn't go any further on the Sinclair Computer, as he had got out of it its full potential. He really wanted a BBC Computer. They were beyond our means at that time but a friend of ours lent him his for a while.

Meanwhile Paul's second year school report read as follows:–

'English: Paul is showing a positive attitude towards his difficulties.

Paul works to the best of his ability.

Paul tries hard but lacks ability.

Paul shows a positive attitude to his work!

And his third year:–

'A pleasing pupil who is good orally, however Paul must make more effort to overcome his difficulties with written work.'

The next two years were to prove very interesting. Paul was improving very gradually, but he was still experiencing difficulty with reading and writing. It took him a long time to focus on any letters or figures. He explained: 'It was as if I had to hold each letter still before I could go on to the next. By the time I got to the next word, I had forgotten the other one so it was very hard to make sense of what I was reading.'

By August 1980, when Paul was thirteen years old, Mr. Norman again reviewed his work and his reading was vastly improved. Then in July 1981, he was top of the year for maths – that is in the whole school year not just the Dyslexic Unit. This was a crucial year as Paul was starting his 'O' level and 'CSE' courses. Also Mrs. Chaudri, head of the Unit, was leaving and being replacd by Mrs. France. So Paul was working to the best of his ability and improving but he still had a big problem with the movement of letters and figures as he tried to focus on them. This constantly daunted him and slowed him down, causing him great frustration. Mr. Norman was very helpful. All through Paul's school years he took time to explain things. When I interviewed him recently, he explained, 'If a child is not learning, the approach to education is wrong. Every child can learn but we must determine the appropriate action. We are not looking at a 'Medical Model'. We make an assessment of strengths and weaknesses to enable us to see what type of educational programme can be used by the child. We need to set the objective to work towards and ensure that the child experiences success.' Mr Norman has very kindly allowed me to publish guidelines he has drawn up.

Some Guidelines for Parents on Helping Children who are Slow in Learning to Read

It is apparent from a great volume of research carried out on pupil's learning in schools that the attitudes of parents, and their ability to motivate and encourage their children, play a very important part in their academic progress. This is even more apparent for those children who have difficulty in acquiring the basic skills of reading. Care should be taken, however, on the way in which these children are supported at home and the type of incentives that they are given. The object of helping children at home is not to teach them to read, but to give them the practice to consolidate skills learned in school and to build up their confidence in, and motivation for, reading. So often, when parents give their children lessons at home this leads to frustration on the part of the parent because of the child's difficulties, and resentment and experience of failure on the part of the children, because they are unable to satisfy their parents' expectations. Teaching reading is a complex skill. The help that parents offer at home should always be in conjunction with the classroom teacher who is responsible for the teaching techniques employed with that child. This will ensure continuity of approach and work geared to the child's interest and ability level.

There are four golden rules which parents should adhere to when helping children with their reading at home:

1. It is essential that the child is given the correct book. If he is failing on more than one word in twenty the book is too difficult for him. Reading should be discontinued and an alternative book found. Equally the book he reads at home should be interesting and stimulating to the child himself. Avoid giving an eight-year-old books geared to a five-year-old's interests.
2. When your child reads to you, the way you correct him when he makes an error affects not only his experience of success with the reading task, but his ability to understand what he is reading. If your child cannot recognise a word or doesn't attempt to build it up, simply tell him the word, even if he has read it correctly in an earlier part of the text. Remember that words take on different meaning depending on the context. If your child reads a word incorrectly, but carries

on reading and the sense of the sentence is lost as a result of his error, wait until the end of the sentence and point out his mistake telling him the correct word. If he misreads a word, but substitutes an appropriate alternative then do not bring this to his attention but allow him to continue reading. All of us when reading efficiently will tend to substitute words with equivalent meaning which enable us to sustain our flow and understanding. Remember also that when pointing out an error to a child the inflection in your voice can reflect the disappointment you feel over his difficulty.

3. After a reading session, which need be no longer than ten to fifteen minutes, it is important to ensure that your child has understood what he has read. Discuss the story or facts with him, and ask him questions which demand some depth of understanding. For example, rather than asking for a single fact such as 'who dropped the glass slipper?', ask a question demanding a deeper level of reasoning, e.g. 'what might have happened if she hadn't dropped the glass slipper?'; 'what do you think will happen next in the story?'; 'what would you like to happen next?'. You can then check that he has understood the progression of events in the text and the consequences of one upon another.
4. At the end of every session always give your child praise and encouragement to build up his own confidence in his reading ability. If you are unable to do this, then you are using the wrong book. You are also failing in the most important role you have to play, that of parent.

These few notes serve to give an outline of the kind of help which would be most beneficial to your child at home. If you find that he does not respond to your interest, it is better to leave the reading for a time altogether, rather than to build up negative attitudes over reading by forcing him to read to you. If you have difficulty in finding an appropriate book for him then consult his class teacher or, failing that, contact your local Educational Psychologist.

P. F. Norman
Senior Educational Psychologist
Beaconsfield Division

10

'The Grass Has Stopped Moving'

THE END OF TERM, July 1981, arrived and this was the school holiday after which Paul would start his 'O' level and CSE courses. Then two years later, in May/June 1983, he would sit his exams.

He had slowly progressed during the past years. His first two years in the Dyslexic Unit had been to him a ray of light in a very long dark tunnel. At last he had people who understood his problem. Even if they didn't understand completely, they were desperately trying to find ways to help him and gain more insight into his specific Learning/Language Difficulty.

The six week summer school holiday was before us and this posed the usual questionings – Did Paul continue working at home during the holiday? He needed a break. He needed to relax. Yet if he did he would be left behind at the beginning of the September term. These next two years were so important. He decided himself that he would rather do some work in the holidays so that he didn't slip behind.

As a family we had planned to go on holiday to the Dales Bible Week in August. At these convention holidays there was always the nagging throught, what will Paul do if he gets asked to read anything? He never even looked at a song sheet it took so long for him to focus on each individual letter. He was very much held back by the movement of the letters. He said, 'It sometimes makes them look as if you're underwater. They all move around and sometimes merge into one.' At this stage we were very much involved with the Baptist Church we attended. We had some lovely times but also experienced much heartache as we tried to bring the fellowship into a renewed freer worship of God. Many of the folks wanted what God was doing, but there was also opposition at times.

Our whole group going on this holiday consisted of over seventy people, including adults, teenagers, children and babies. It was a real family affair and very exciting for the children and teenagers. Our particular camp consisted of a large marquee for eating, a smaller one for cooking in, about fifteen frame tents for sleeping and two caravans. Andy and I were fortunate to have a caravan! We worked it well! Paul and Barry were in the tents with the other young people and Ruth shared the caravan with us.

Camping to me always seems like hard work. This was different, indeed quite luxurious! We were very well organised and had rotas for cooking, collecting water, emptying slops, shopping and washing the kitchen utensils after the meals. Each table was responsible for their own washing up. So it meant that mothers who normally cooked at home would only be on cooking duty for one meal during the week, but that would be for seventy people. Everybody had jobs to do, even the children. It worked very well.

The evening sessions were mainly for adults but teenagers could attend if they wished. There were other arrangements for teenagers and children. The morning sessions were divided into different areas, teenagers, children, creche, leaders, family life, money, and so on. So each person attended the one appropriate to his own interest. We hardly saw the kids during the week as there was always something for them to do or someone to talk to.

After one of the morning seminars, Andy and I were in our caravan when Paul appeared at the door. He looked as if he had had a fright or something. At the same time he was so excited. 'I've been healed!' he exclaimed. 'You've been what!' we replied together. 'Healed!' he said. 'The letters have all stopped moving. Even the grass has stopped moving!'

We were speechless. We didn't know what to do. We wanted to hug him, dance, shout to everyone on the camp. On the other hand, we were rather shocked. We had prayed all these years for God to step in but was it really true? Paul continued, 'As I went in the tent I knew that God was going to do something for me. People were going out to the front to be prayed for, but I didn't. I raised my hands and began to worship God. Across the front of the tent in big letters was written 'ONE WAY WITH JESUS'. Before I closed my eyes, the letters were moving up and down and going around and around. I felt as if my mind was going mad as I stood there with all these letters moving around so quickly in my head. But when I opened my eyes, they had all stopped moving.' As he came out of the tent he exclaimed to the other teenagers with him, 'Even the grass has stopped moving!'

11

The Dyslexic Unit

WHAT A PRIVILEGE it is to live in a world where God is personally interested in those who want to know. This particular touch from Him and Paul's life changed dramatically. His February 1982 school report read:

English Language B+
Maths A−
Conduct and attitude – Excellent.
And in July 1982:
English Language A−
Maths A−
Chemistry B
Biology B
Comment: 'It is clear that Paul has made considerable efforts in all his subjects with satisfactory results. A very good year's work. Well done!'

Remember Paul hadn't been entered for CSE English exam, but part way through the course in summer 1982 the school telephoned us to say that he was overtaking some of the pupils who were taking the exams and they felt he should be allowed to take not only English Language but also English Literature. We could hardly believe what we heard! This meant we would have to pay for Paul because the school hadn't recommended him as a candidate at the official time of entry. Of course we didn't mind. We would have done anything for him to succeed.

Mrs. France, who was now the teacher in charge of the Unit, explained to me – 'This will mean that Paul will have to work really hard. He is highly motivated but we are all amazed at the marked improvement in his work. I am surprised at the confidence which he has developed since Sept 1981.' She went on to explain, 'This will mean Paul having to write five essays for the English Language exam and fifteen essays for the English Literature exam.' This was amazing when we thought of Paul's problems eighteen months earlier. We hadn't realised how severe the problem had been. The grass to him had looked like a mass of velvet constantly moving. As he watched television, tried to read books, looked at pictures and tried to write, everything was moving. Imagine how tired it would make one trying to focus on constantly moving objects.

For the next two days Paul was quite delirious and had a high temperature. So much so that he moved into the caravan with us, and we had to have the camp doctor in to see him. It was quite strange. We don't fully understand whether it was the shock of what happened to him or not.

By the next day the news had raced around the camp. There were many people who knew Paul and loved him. Bryn Jones, whom we have known for many years, asked me if I would share what had happened in the Leaders Seminar. I tried to volunteer Andy but Bryn said he would like to hear from the mother's heart. It was beautiful just sharing with a hundred leaders and their wives what God had done. We were yet to see the outworking and result of this miracle.

During that afternoon the Yorkshire Radio Reporter came to our caravan to interview Paul. His temperature was still high but he wanted to tell them what God had done. The reporter took Paul's Bible, opened it at Chronicles and asked Paul to read the chapter. Andy stood back in silence waiting. Then Paul began steadily and without hesitation he read through the whole chapter. Without a hitch! That sure was a miracle! We knew that something had happened to Paul, but couldn't really understand with our human minds the full extent of what had taken place.

About three days after this miracle, still on the camp site, I was walking across the grass to our caravan and God spoke to me about our local church. It was in vision form but also in word. I saw letters, some straight, some lying on their side, some upside down and others constantly moving. God said 'My church looks like this. It gives an unclear picture to those who look at her. It is confusing. In this miracle I have caused these letters to stand up straight and be seen clearly – you, my people, I want to arise and give a clear picture to those who observe your presence.' I felt that God was using Paul as an example. He wanted a clear image portrayed to the world. We were a little apprehensive going home, although Paul was full of confidence. He knew that he had encountered the living God. We wondered what to tell the teachers, the psychologist, the doctors! We knew that God had touched Paul but we wanted to be a little bit careful!

What we didn't want Paul to do was to go back to school and tell the staff in the Unit that he didn't need them anymore! Andy advised Paul that it was better to go back to school and work hard, and wait for them to notice. He had a lot of catching up to do, especially with his spelling. He did this, but after about three weeks his maths teacher asked him what had happened. She had heard in a round about way of his healing. When interviewing the teachers recently, they said they stood back in amazement and watched with sheer delight how his confidence and motivation grew. His work level progressed so quickly and his reading took off. It was as we thanked God in the family that we came into the realisation of what had happened. It surely was a miracle! We wanted to share it with the wider church but we were told not to at the moment.

One of the elders cried when Andy shared it with him. Many members of the congregation rejoiced with us, but somehow there was a holding back. What if God hasn't really done it? Paul was very faithful and trusted God completely. Before he would never look at a song sheet or hymn book, even if one was offered to him.

One particular morning, about two weeks after this miracle, the preacher asked for somebody to read some particular verses out of the Bible. Paul was the first one up. He read confidently, clearly and fluently. Andy and I looked at each other with tears streaming down our faces. We never really believed that we would see this moment, it was so beautiful. It was only possible because God had stepped in and caused the letters and the grass to stop moving!

One of Paul's teachers at the Dyslexic Unit of Pembroke School has written the following report of her association with Paul and his progress:

> I joined the staff of the Dyslexia Unit (as it was called then) in 1980, employed specifically to develop the teaching of mathematics to those children who were having problems handling numbers and mathematical concepts. Nationally, it has been shown that about 72 per cent of all children having specific learning difficulties have numeracy problems as well as literacy ones, and this has been our experience at Pembroke.
>
> However, I did not encounter Paul as a pupil for some time because he was coping well with maths lessons in the main school. But quite soon I began to be involved with the Christian Union at Pembroke and found Paul to be a valued member of the group, always making a useful contribution and eventually taking up a leadership role in his final year. Paul was always open and forthright about his faith in God but also showed sensitivity where necessary. Naturally, I began to take a particular interest in

Paul, especially as I was supporting him in some of his main school courses, and found him to be both intelligent and conscientious but having a severe problem in communicating his thoughts on paper.

So, it was really thrilling when Paul returned after the long summer holiday in 1981 and told me that he had been healed of his Dyslexia. He asked me not to say anything to his teachers as it seemed better that they should discover what had happened for themselves. Indeed it took only weeks for several members of staff to comment about the improvement in Paul's written work and this was confirmed and highlighted for us firstly by the psychologist's report that year and then by satisfactory examination results. Educationally, Paul's healing wasn't instant in the sense that he could write immediately like other intelligent boys of the same age, but the healing was the start of a rapid learning process in spelling, punctuation and the logical presentation of thoughts on paper.

When Paul transferred to the College of Further Education in High Wycombe. I was delighted to be the one assigned to monitor and assist him if necessary, as he remained a 'statemented' pupil under the 1981 Education Act and as such was entitled to support whilst in full-time education up to the age of nineteen. I contacted the Special Needs Tutor at the College (Mr. Royce) who put me in contact with Paul's course tutor, Mr. Watts. On my first visit to Mr. Watts, I explained carefully the sort of problems that students with specific learning difficulties have and asked him to alert me if it seemed necessary to give Paul regular support in the way I was already doing for Robert, another pupil from Paul's year who was studying in the sixth form of a local grammar school. Since

I didn't hear anything from Mr. Watts in the following weeks and Paul himself assured me that all was going well, I returned to the College towards the end of term. Mr. Watts showed me some of Paul's work, which still showed some dyslexic tendencies, but he assured me that Paul's spelling was comparable with others on the course and that his grasp of the work was more than satisfactory. My visits became less frequent and phone calls to Mr. Watts and to Paul became all that were necessary. On Monday, 4th February 1985, I rang Mr. Watts for a half-yearly report and found myself being questioned by him about whether Paul had really had the specific learning difficulty that I had described on our first meeting, since Paul was now an exceptional student who was likely to progress to higher education. I assured Mr. Watts of the accuracy of what I had said but reminded him that Paul believed himself healed by God, a view that I also shared. Mr. Watts agreed that the facts supported this.

(signed) Kathryn Morgan

Meanwhile, during that very special year, Paul was progressing rapidly in his skills with his computer. And it was clear that he needed a more advanced model. After some discussion between us we decided we would go for a Dragon Computer, not nearly as good as a BBC but a lot more memory than the Sinclair. Paul was delighted and worked hard on it. He had been using an old black and white TV with his Sinclair, but the Dragon needed a colour TV. People felt for Paul and he was a thankful kid and was easily satisfied. He carried on with the black and white TV without moaning or complaining until one of our dearest friends, Marion, who is like a big sister to the kids and lived with us when we had the extended family, gave Paul her nice coloured TV. It meant so much to him he could now really excel with graphics which he was longing to do.

By this time Paul was fourteen years old. He had the choice of doing two weeks full time work experience which the school would arrange at an appropriate place, or the pupil could find one themselves. Paul approached one of the young men who worked at a computer firm in Reading called 'Candella Instruments'. He said he would look at the possibilities but his firm hadn't had people so young on work experience before. When the answer came it was 'yes' it was going to be possible. Paul was delighted, so were the school as they hadn't got a child from the Dyslexia Unit into a computer firm before. He travelled to and from Reading with Brett each morning. Brett explained to me recently, 'It was hard monotonous work Paul was doing on the computers but he was excellent. He tackled the job until it was completed. We still use the work he has done. He's very good on computers.' At the end of his work experience the boss gave him a nice gift of money and he was thrilled.

Before Paul's experience at the Dales week in August, he had been giving thought to the subjects he should take at 'O' level standard. We wept for him, we prayed for him, we spent time with him listening to his endless conversation, we praised him, we gave him responsibility, we told him he was precious to us exactly how he was – but how was this going to help him through his exams?

The pupils in the Dyslexia Unit were never entered for CSE English Language exam and definitely not English Literature. Paul, the teachers, the Psychologist, and ourselves had talked for a considerable time about the 'options' Paul should pursue. He had always been good at maths, which was unusual as many children with specific learning difficulty have problems with the computational side of maths. He enjoyed Chemistry, Biology, Technical Drawing and Pottery/Woodwork. He was entered for his choices but of course these didn't include English.

Then, suddenly and quite dramatically, the letters stopped moving, and from this stage he literally 'took

The Elga Group

Schools Competition

'Water–What is it?'

This is to certify that

PAUL CROALL

of

THE PEMBROKE SCHOOL (DYSLEXIC UNIT)

School

Came THIRD in our

Water Competition

This Scroll was presented by

Roy Castle

on the 23rd October 1981

Signed

off'. We were delighted when, in October 1981, he was presented with a prize by Roy Castle for producing a project on 'The Water Supply'. It was excellent. He, along with another pupil from the Unit, had worked so hard and so much detail had been included in the project, so much research was carried out and so much writing needed – it was a real joy for us and the staff from the school who all attended the Presentation.

How we thanked God that, at last, Paul was making rapid progress in all his subjects.

The following was written in his school report in December 1982, one year and one term after 'the grass stopped moving.'

> *Language Development:* Paul's work has continued to improve throughout the term. His written work shows marked progress in spelling and punctuation. I am delighted with the way he is so obviously enjoying the challenge of more demanding work. All his work is steadily improving in quality. His CSE English Mock results are well deserved. Well done!
> *English Language and Literature:* Paul has approached our in-depth reading of '*Animal Farm*' with great maturity, and has achieved an impressive understanding of the political and social levels of the story as well as having a solid grasp of the story line. His oral contributions show fluency, and he is generally both confident and sensitive in arguing his point, being able to stand his ground against counter arguments, but also being willing to listen to other points of view. His work on vocabulary extension and comprehension have both been satisfactory, and his written answers are now showing greater accuracy. His decision to take the CSE English Literature paper next year shows his increased confidence, and he seems to be enjoying the

challenge of working under the pressure of a heavy work load.

Assessment: Paul is making excellent progress.

Mr. Norman, the Educational Psychologist, carried out tests during that year and reported that Paul had 'much improved.'

In September 1982 we saw Mr. Norman again. He carried out more tests on Paul; he records: 'Much Improved'.

In April 1983 we received a letter from Mr. Norman, enclosing an article on 'Binocular Instability'. This was the part of Paul's problem that had really held him back. When he looked at anything, including letters and figures, they kept on moving. Imagine the effort a child has to put into focusing, and how tiring it must be for a child to see like this! Mr. Norman felt that his important role in Paul's life was to get people together; headteachers, teachers, remedial teachers, parents and Paul. He wanted to alert people to Paul's special needs, he wanted to shed light on the situation. He feels that the role of the parent is very important but they should not become teachers. I asked him about Paul suddenly and quite dramatically taking off from the age of fourteen years. Paul had talked to him about the dramatic experience he had had whilst on holiday. Mr. Norman acknowledged that, if a person has faith and the environment is right, then things can happen. He explained to me that the movement of letters and figures that Paul experienced could be associated with weakness in the eye muscles, which mature and strengthen over the years. Was it a late maturation of the muscle? I questioned further. One moment the letters were moving and the next they had stopped and from that point Paul really took off. To me it is significant that the movement stopped at that point. He explained to me: 'It is like someone coming to Christ or falling in love; it may have been happening over a period, but one day there is the moment of realisation.' I asked, was it to do with the therapy he was receiving? But it wasn't, it was quite miraculous. I asked about the medical viewpoint that suggested that Paul would never do anything academically. He observed that he had not held that view but hadn't expected Paul to get on so well.

We are really thankful for the help and instruction we have received on Paul's account from the educational psychologist. He left no avenue unexplored that would possibly help Paul overcome his difficulties. It has been a joy to have his involvement in our lives and for the part he played in Paul's healing we are grateful.

One of the ways Mr. Norman had helped was to have Paul made a Subject of Statement to get into Pembroke School and the Dyslexia Unit. To be a Subject of Statement meant that Mr. Norman had written to the examining Board of the school, suggesting that Paul should be given certain concessions to protect his educational needs. These included someone to work alongside Paul in his exams to read the questions to him and write down his answers. But, when it came to the CSE and 'O' levels exams, Paul did not want any of these concessions, he wanted to do it on his own. We could have persuaded him to have help, but we knew that he now was aware of what he could do and wanted to compete like the other children in the school. As soon as he was released from his reading problem, Paul wanted to be treated as any other young person. But there was one big difference. He had a great desire to help others and also the ability to do so. It was during these years that he negotiated to deal with Avon Social Service. He has designed four programmes for them to use in helping children with differing handicaps. One which intrigues me is 'Time Warpers'. It's used to help children get places but to do this they have to get help from their colleagues. It is a mass of caves and the aim is to get out of the caves but you may have to ask your friend for help with a hook or rope. It's very exciting and helps children who have difficulty communicating with others to use other people's skills. Very interesting, as Paul fully understands the feeling. He calls his range of software 'Solomon's Software'.

Through Peter Norman he was introduced to two teachers in Milton Keynes who specialise in educational programmes. We have been amazed at Paul's confidence. He telephoned these men and arranged to take over his software to demonstrate. Andy and I took him over by car and left him. The teachers said he would be about three quarters of an hour. When we arrived back, they were deep into computer technology. We had to give them another hour.

The need for a BBC computer was becoming more apparent. So was the need for Barry to have a motor bike and Ruth a saxophone. We desperately needed a new car! All the time we had to weigh up the necessities and not ignore Barry and Ruth's needs.

Paul worked hard at his 'O' levels and CSEs. We had looked at all the local colleges including Slough, Amersham, Uxbridge and High Wycombe. There was a variety of courses offered. He knew he wanted to go on the National B. Tech. Diploma Course but he needed four 'O' levels and some required English 'O' level. At each interview they said he would be able to get in on the basic computer course for which no 'O' levels were necessary. He was well past this computer course, although he had been retarded in other areas. During the school holidays he worked sometimes voluntarily at Hillingdon Social Services. He did some valuable work designing programmes for mentally handicapped children. Although Paul wasn't being paid for this, he was gaining experience.

There was still much interest in the possible medical causes which could affect a child with SLD – Specific Learning Difficulty – and, in April 1983, Mrs. France realised there may be a problem with the hearing of some of these children. Paul's hearing had been checked years before and appeared alright, but she encouraged parents to give their permission for the pupils to have a pure-tone audiometric test – here is the result of Paul's test:

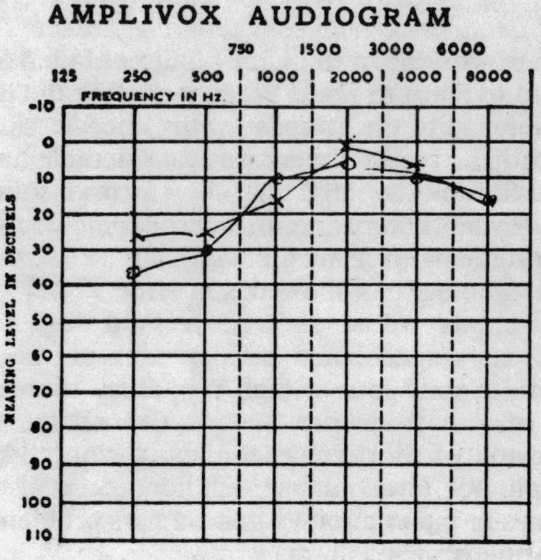

Pure tone audiometric tests

I am enclosing details of the above test concerning your son's hearing.

A straight line between 0–10 is normal hearing; 15–30 shows moderate loss; 35–40 shows severe loss.

The loss of low frequency sounds involves:

g, m, b, d, r, w, l.

a, e, i, o, u.

These results have confirmed the need to use a multi-sensory approach in teaching your son, but we are exploring educational implications of the test results and will contact you with further information when it is available.

Please do not hesitate to contact me if you wish to discuss the test results.

Yours sincerely,
B. France.

Mrs. France explained to me about the hearing problems in this report.

Prior to working in the Unit I had not failed to help a child to learn to read. When analysing the literacy problems of the pupils with specific learning difficulties I realised there was considerable auditory confusion mostly affecting short vowel sounds in single-syllable words, confusion of some consonants and problems with word endings.

The audiograms showed that over 90 per cent of Unit pupils tested showed a mild loss of low frequency sounds; and 50 per cent of the pupils showed a mild loss of high frequency sounds. The loss of low frequency sounds contributes to the confusion of short-vowel sounds in words like pat, pet, pit, pot, put; and flap, flip, flop, etc. It also helps to confuse b and d sounds: and causes problems with low sounds such as l, m, v, etc.

The loss of high frequency sounds contributes to difficulties with ch and sh; confusion of d on the low frequencies with t on the high frequencies, etc.

Successful teaching methods with pupils with specific reading difficulties need to make allowances for the degree of auditory confusion especially of low frequency sounds. Paul's written work and spelling displayed confusion of these types. Because of the problems of auditory confusion the use of phonics in the teaching of reading causes considerable difficulties for most of the pupils referred to the Unit. Most of the pupils were taught to read quickly and efficiently using visual and sound matching techniques.

About one in ten of the pupils in the Unit had severe visual matching problems. These pupils had much greater difficulties to overcome and responded much more slowly. A multi-sensory dimension had to be added to the work to help pupils with this degree of difficulty. Pupils need to see, hear, say and write what they are learning.

Paul needed stimulating work with depth and challenge, plus wide reading experience. Whilst good quality literature should be read, it is important to include a range of technical material right from the beginning of secondary education, and earlier if possible, to compensate for the years of reading failure.

Paul showed an appreciation and enjoyment of literature, drama and poetry. He responded with pleasure to quite complex material, enjoying the stimulus and displaying insight and understanding. Once when I was reading the "Rhyme of the Ancient Mariner" with Paul, I stopped and asked him if he was finding it boring, but he immediately pushed the enquiry aside saying it was quite involved, but he was intrigued by the story and wanted to know what happened next.

When I first taught Paul he was hesitant and lacked confidence when reading aloud. When reading silently to himself he displayed a good level of comprehension. In his written work his sentence structure and spelling were weak. Paul was of middle ability, but well motivated. I did not regard him as one of our most able pupils.

Pupils in the Unit are all statemented as having average and above-average potential. Some of the Unit pupils would be grammar school pupils were it not for their specific learning difficulties. (Bucks has a twelve plus exam to identify academically able pupils; Paul was in a Unit linked with a secondary modern school which took the pupils who did not pass their twelve plus.) I regarded Paul as middle ability. His language processing problems were of the type that would continue to present problems and would probably prevent him from producing good quality work.

From 1982 there has been a noticeable change in Paul's work. I have been surprised by the improvement in his confidence. His emerging self-confidence and his determination caused him steadily to overtake pupils with higher ability. He was always optimistic and well motivated. There was a vast improvement in his written and oral English over the two years I knew him. He had a quiet confidence in God. When Paul knew he was being entered for the CSE English Language exam unassisted, it had a marked effect on the standard of his written work and his motivation. It was quite dramatic. We sat back in amazement at the progress he made. Not only did he take CSE English Language unassisted, but he also took CSE English Literature, preparing for the exam in a very short time. Here again his work steadily improved. Suddenly at the time when the folders of written assignments were due for handing in, we realised that Paul's literature file was incomplete: a further 2,000 word assignment was required. We explained the problem and Paul sat down quietly and worked until he had completed the assignment. He was just somehow being driven on. He gained a Grade 2 CSE in English Language and a Grade 2 CSE English Literature. This was a miracle. None of his teachers had expected Paul to obtain such high grades.

Mrs. France explained the change in motivation of some of the Unit pupils when she decided to enter them for the CSE English Language exam with which they could not have the help of an amanuensis. Even barely literate pupils' work improved quite dramatically. The standard of their written work just changed completely over a relatively short period once they had an exam to work for.

She also talked about the importance of parental involvement with their children's work. Where there is a good working relationship between parents and teachers, the pupil's work benefits and they work harder. Without parental co-operation pupils make less consistent progress. She felt that the home and parents are the most important influence in a pupil's educational progress. In some cases of severe reading failure, involving a loss of confidence and co-operation from the pupil, the combined efforts of the parents and teachers have proved successful. Very often in these severe cases a pupil can appear to be working, but is, in fact, ignoring the guidelines given and simply not following instructions and routines. When these non-conforming pupils are identified and full parental support given, the pupil then finds his reading skills developing, his confidence improves and very soon everyone can see the difference.

12

On To Higher Education

IN MARCH 1983, the Careers Officer came to Pembroke School and Paul expressed his desire to go on a computer course at college. For this he would need four 'O' levels or equivalent.

At this time there was no provision for a child with specific learning difficulties to stay on at the Dyslexia Unit for an 'A' level course, so we wrote to the education offices about this and they advised us to contact the local grammar school. We did this and Paul, Andy and I had an interview with the headmaster, who was prepared to accept Paul for an 'A' level course if he passed four subjects at 'O' level or the equivalent CSEs. But Paul had decided he would prefer college life and to study for the National B. Tech. Computer Course. His decision was right and we learned that you can only guide your child and help them in their decisions, but then must be right behind them in their choice. It doesn't work to be negative and criticise them, 'If only you had done what I said!'

Paul gained three 'O' levels. He sat all his exams without receiving the help that he could have had as a Statemented pupil. He turned down the offer for somebody to read his exam papers to him and also for somebody to write down his answers – we were apprehensive but it was his decision.

He applied to the college knowing that he was one 'O' level short – but he was determined that that was what he should do. He had to sit an entrance exam and we prayed so much for him because he would have been devastated had he not got in. It took about ten days for the result to come through and it seemed like an eternity. Eventually the letter came to say that he was accepted, and he was delighted and full of determination to do well.

So in September 1983, Paul started on his National B. Tech. Diploma Course at Bucks College of Higher Education, High Wycombe. He started off at the bottom of the group, as his English was so far behind that of the others, but by the end of the second year he was in the top three.

In April 1984, when Paul was nearing the end of his first year at college, he was still 'Statemented' under the 1981 Education Act. We received a letter from the Dyslexia Unit asking if Paul could be 'de-Statemented'. It reads:

> We have had an excellent interim report on Paul's progress: the college are very satisfied with his work and feel he is more than holding his own in the course.
>
> Because of his progress we would now like to have your consent and approval before we proceed with de-statementing. We would hope to have this completed by about the middle of the autumn term so that we can satisfy ourselves that there are no hiccoughs in the transition from first to second year.
>
> If you feel this would be appropriate at this stage would you let me have your approval in writing? Do not hesitate to state any reservations you may have – for instance de-statementing will remove any remaining privileges under the 1981 Education Act, e.g. free, full-time education up to the age of nineteen, but will not in any way interfere with his normal rights to further education – it will simply remove him from our support.
>
> We have just started a Unit prayer link for circulation amongst our Christian friends. I am enclosing

a copy – we would greatly appreciate your continued fellowship in prayer. We feel it is very important to develop these links at present, as we are about to enter a very unsettling period of two or three years leading up to the re-organisation of secondary education in Wycombe – so do pray for us and our work.

Best wishes,

(Signed) Mrs. C. France,
The Dyslexia Unit,
The Pembroke School.

Mrs. France has much wisdom and experience in teaching and working with children with Specific Learning/Language Difficulties. I thank God that she was available to Paul, Andy and me during some very hard years. She and the other members of the staff played a very important role in Paul's healing – I thank them from the bottom of my heart.

She has kindly prepared an audio cassette and leaflet on 'How to Help Your Child with Language', also Mrs. Catherine Morgan has prepared a cassette and leaflet on 'How to Help your Child with Learning Difficulties in Maths.' They are both available at small cost. Mrs. Morgan is a very experienced and caring member of the staff at the Unit; she has kept a lovely watch on Paul even while he has been at college.

Halfway through Paul's first year at college we decided that our next step should be to buy a BBC Computer. This would help us all, I needed a typewriter, so we would get word processing facilities on it. Barry liked playing computer games. Paul always says he makes the games and Barry plays them! Ruth enjoys making music on the computer and typing her poems. Andy puts his accounts and church affairs into it. Much to my surprise – I use it! I never thought it possible because they used to frighten me, but Paul has been so patient teaching us all how to get the best out of the computer and, of course, Paul has benefited greatly himself.

Marion again bought Paul a compatible tape recorder for his birthday present – this was really good. The need for a disc arose and we looked again. Yes, it was so important. What about a printer? It's so infuriating if you have all this lovely work and can't print it. To use it as a typewriter it was a necessity. So we invested in a printer. All very worthwhile but very expensive.

For part of Paul's college work he did a project at our local doctor's surgery. He designed a package for them. Also he evaluated a number of available packages designed for doctors to assist them in their practice with regard to client data base and medication and contra-indications. He got a glowing report from the doctors concerned.

It was a very exciting time. Suddenly, after all the pain and heartache, here was Paul taking off. As Roger Carter, his college teacher, said, 'This shows a student who has been retarded and suddenly taken off.' His second and final year at Wycombe College, he went from the bottom part of the group to the top part. His final report reads 'Excellent progress.' He also said 'I am delighted with Paul's high standard of programming and the lack of difficulty with written work. Paul is one of the most able students in the group – I have written a good reference for Paul for University or Polytechnic, but I feel he will succeed whatever the result of these applications.'

Mrs. France, the teacher-in-charge of the Department for Children with Specific Learning Difficulties, kindly agreed to talk to me about Paul and his education while I prepared this book. The words she used to describe the improvement in Paul's work stunned me: 'Dramatic', 'Amazed', 'Sheer delight', 'Amazed at response', 'Excited with progress' and 'Sitting back in amazement at the progress he had made'. She said: 'I have been amazed and surprised at the reports I have had back. Having regarded Paul as a well motivated but fairly mediocre pupil, the report of his success at college made it increasingly obvious that he was reaching a far higher academic level than I would have thought possible.' As Paul got nearer to the end of his course at Wycombe College, he designed a programme to act as a dictionary and correct his spellings for him.

Through his teenage years, he had always been very thoughtful and helpful to other children who suffered from similar problems. I can remember him spending time with Bradley, Nicky, Ryan and particularly Mark. Mark was from a family which wasn't very well off. Paul sat with him at the computer for three hours a week to help him learn. When he was leaving for college he arranged for an older Dragon Computer (which he paid towards) to be accessible to Mark. He so wants to help children who have experienced any kind of problems. We know that what we have invested in his life – time, energy, praise, communication (it takes time!) and money has been worth it and is still worth it. He is precious to us all.

Have you ever stood back, looked at yourself and wondered 'Am I an over protective parent?' 'Do I expose my children to hard situations and guide them through gently, or do I hide them and protect them from hard times, negative attitudes, violence and crime?' Life is very hard; on the TV and in newspapers we hear of violence, war, killing, rape and children missing. It is a horrible world into which our children are born. In the beginning the whole creation was beautiful but man, through his sin and greed, has brought about such deprivation. It really saddens me to see children becoming hardened to murder, evil and crime. They have to in a way to protect themselves but somehow we, as parents, have a very difficult task. We don't want to expose our offspring to everything that is shown on film and video, but, on the other hand, we don't want to over protect them or we will lead them into a fantasy world. It is a very difficult job, we need constantly to assess our own attitudes, the way we live and what we watch and condone on TV.

Often around our dining room table we spend time talking about life, school, sex, lovemaking, teachers' attitudes and many other topical subjects. Some of our visitors are a little embarrassed at how open our teenagers are. We have always felt the need for honesty. It is very easy to shut children up because of our own embarrassment, maybe we don't know all the answers. They don't mind that, in fact they will respect you if you admit you haven't an answer but will try to find out for them.

As we observe our youngsters, do we feel the visitors have a greater influence on their lives than our example does? Sometimes Andy and I just sit, watch and listen to our three teenagers in conversation with their friends or our friends, maybe on the telephone or face to face. We realise that in Paul, Barry and Ruth, God is operating. We have to be careful not to squash what they say and not to dismiss it. I tell you we don't always find it easy.

When parents are popular and in great demand from other people, it can inhibit children from expressing their own character. They can become very much overshadowed by a dad who is very much in the public eye, and a mum who lots of people come to for counselling and help.

Our son Barry is a real handsome six-footer who has always been very bright and quick at school. His main ambition at the moment is to get a big motorbike to replace his 50cc moped. In actual fact he has everything going for him. He sings and plays the guitar in the music group at church, has a pretty girl friend and many other friends.

One sad thing we had been aware of with Barry is that he had difficulty expressing his own opinion. This may have been linked to Paul with his handicap, although we had gone out of our way to ensure that

Barry and Ruth were not left out in any way. Paul had always needed to talk and he did! Whereas Barry was the younger brother and was sometimes squashed by Paul. I saw this difficulty in Barry and the agony he felt which brought to me the same pain I felt about Paul's handicap. I wanted him to be free to be himself, to speak out, without fear of being put down or not heard.

It took quite a few tearful conversations with all the family to sort this one out. It was no use just telling Barry to open his mouth and not to be so sensitive. We had to encourage Paul to be quiet at times and let Barry express his opinion. Barry had been bugged by this for some time but at a holiday one Easter a breakthrough occurred. Barry, Ruth and Paul went on a youth holiday with other teenagers from the church. One of the youth leaders encouraged Barry to be himself and to share with his friends how he felt. He was always 'Andy Croall's son'. Even on holiday after just being counselled, he came out of the chalet and a girl introduced him to her friend as 'Andy Croall's son.' He was really shattered but later was able to confront the young lady about it, whereas in the past he would have just taken it and shrivelled inside.

So he shared his feeling with the youth leader, then his girl friend and her friend, and then at home with me while a friend of mine was visiting. As he shared his feelings the burden became lighter and he spoke with greater freedom from his feelings. He talked to me for about thirty minutes about his hurts. Later Andy, Paul and Ruth joined us and he went through it all again. It was painful but as he shared it and expressed those deep feelings it became easier. As we listened and prayed with Barry, God spoke into my mind and spirit a very special word which was right from God's Spirit for Barry. It was that God had chosen Barry to become a man of authority and a man of courage, and he wanted Barry to take upon himself that authority which was from God himself. Our lounge was hushed as this sunk right into Barry's being, it had reached somewhere that we, as parents, could not reach.

The following Sunday morning, at worship, Barry was playing his guitar in the music group and as usual kept well hidden behind it! The worship leader asked if there was anybody who wanted to share about what God had done for them and about four people got up. Suddenly out of the corner of my eye I saw Barry moving. My heart sank although I was delighted. Here was this sixteen-year-old in front of his dad, whom everybody looks up to, the other elders, his mum, Paul, Ruth, his friends and all the church. He explained to them the agony he felt because people just treated him as Andy Croall's son. He told them that it really hurt him and how God had shown him He loved him as 'Barry', as a real person. I think the whole church were holding back the tears when they realised the pressure that children of leaders experience.

Barry (or Bas as we call him) is a lovely chap who portrays strength and gentleness. To see him with toddlers is beautiful, they all love him, he has got a very fine physique and curly hair. He plans to study dentistry at one of the London hospitals, if he achieves the right grades in his 'A' levels! Whatever he does, we know that God has picked him out as 'special' and He has a perfect plan for his life. We love him very much but God loves him even more.

I have tried to show you that, even when there is pain in a family, God's love is still there. Because there is pain, God hasn't left us, He wants to see us through the pain and see His perfect plan for our lives and that of our children. He knew the pain of a suffering Son and yet He knew what the outcome of the suffering would be. It would be to put an end to Satan, his evil and lies; to forgive us and cleanse us from our sin. This would give us a new start in life and then He would give us the power of the Holy Spirit to live and work through us.

13

'The Sky Is The Limit'

PAUL STUDIED at the Bucks College of Higher Education for two years. His tutor, Mr. Roger Carter, who taught Paul for four lessons per week over these two years, remembered that at the beginning of the course he doubted that Paul would make the grade. His English was so poor and behind the standard of the class and he was considered to be among those at the bottom of the class. Yet, in the two years of study, he progressed to be in the top three. Mr. Carter explained:

> He is the student who has progressed the most in the whole of my teaching career, that is over ten years now. From the start to the end of the course, Paul has been consistently conscientious and contented, but he was a different student at the end of the course than he was at the beginning. His personality hasn't changed but his giftedness has. He started off well below average and I taught him quantitative methods in the first year and one aspect of computing in the second year. Mathematically he began as a rather weak student and certainly his English was very weak. So far as the area he has chosen to pursue is concerned, he is now quite exceptionally good and I would say gifted in that area. No doubt if he had chosen another area, say mathematics, he would have been very good at that also. Yes, at the end of the two years, I would say he was

gifted but I wouldn't have said that at the start, although you have to have reasonable educational attainments to be accepted. Looking back, Paul was obviously an intelligent boy who had been retarded.

Paul struck me as a very happy student, although at the start he was verbally immature. He used to sit apart from the others and not mix. At the end of the two years, he was fully integrated and his ability could match any other.

I never observed he was under stress and when, in the first year, he was rather slow in his mathematics he remained conscientious, slow, but not stressed.

He didn't have a close relationship with the others. The group was a lively bright group that worked very hard but would mess about in a harmless kind of way. Paul didn't have time for that. He had a sense of humour but his attitudes were quite different. Paul used to mess about on the computer and devise all sorts of programmes and send messages to other people's parts of the network. Paul has very strong Christian principles and this also separated him a little from the group.

A person like Paul, as he was then, would obviously prefer to communicate with a machine rather than with people, having a desire to communicate but a feeling of being inadequate and using a substitute. Being an intelligent person and having problems with writing and reading, he could find fulfilment in a computer which he couldn't with other activities. Computers are inherently quite interesting in that, in a computer, there is a lot to unravel. It presents interesting problems so, if you are a problem solving person, a computer is ideal. Finally there is a lot of money to be made in computers. I don't know which applied to Paul, maybe they all did; he obviously found he could handle computers.

As parents we had heard Paul say he wanted to study

for a degree and then to use his expertise after he had progressed as far as possible academically. We had played it a bit cool and felt he was aiming too high. Roger Carter confirmed that, when Paul started his course two years ago, an assessment then would never have seen Paul as a degree student, as only the top two or three in a college course of Further Education are considered for university.

> I must repeat that I see more improvement in Paul than in any other student that I have taught,' stressed the tutor. 'He was a likeable lad who would tend to stay behind to chat and probably related better to the teaching staff than he did to his class. I have no doubt that he has the ability to obtain a good degree and beyond that the sky is really the limit. He strikes me as someone who will grab opportunities and succeed. That's the key and he has everything going for him in that sense. He's seriously minded, intelligent, has application and opportunism. He is very interested in exploring ways of applying computer technology to the needs of the handicapped and as he is so good at programming there will certainly be opportunities in that field. He is remarkable for a person of his age in that he is prepared to see something through to its conclusion, whilst a lot of youngsters start off enthusiastically but dry up and don't complete a project if the going gets tough.

Paul completed the course in July 1985 with credits in all five subjects and a distinction overall. The five subjects were:

Programming Concepts
Cobol Project
Cobol Language
Small Business Systems Concepts
Small Business Systems Practice

We never anticipated he would do so well academically, but hoped for his sake that he might, as he is an intelligent young man who has faced many difficulties and frustrations earlier in his education.

This letter with the news of his success was sent to the Dyslexia Unit:

Mr G. R. Watts
School of Business Studies
Bucks College of Higher Education
High Wycombe,
Bucks

Dear Mrs Morgan

Paul Croall

You will be pleased to hear that Paul achieved a Pass with Distinction in the final round of examinations for his B. Tec. National Diploma in Computer Studies, obtaining a maximum 5 credits.

This will no doubt assist him in his taking a place on one or other of the degree courses for which he has applied.

His general word control has improved considerably. The only query now is in his handwriting standard and he has been advised to concentrate on this during the summer vacation. Not that this would be too destructive as he is a skilled keyboard operator so should be able to do a good portion of his in course assessed work via word processing facilities!

We are all extremely pleased with him and consider his natural ability in his chosen field will overcome his slight disability.

Yours sincerely,
(Signed) G. R. Watts
Course Co-ordinator,
B. Tec. N.D. Comp. Studies

We did a lot of heart searching, shed a lot of tears, sought a lot of professional help, but today Paul can read as well as anybody. He still spells some words incorrectly, although phonetically correct. You see, he never learnt how to spell: the teachers and ourselves were more concerned just to enable Paul to write. His spelling improves every day.

Parents, please don't give up on your children or push them so hard that they feel failures, but rather speak into their lives positive attitudes. In later years you will be grateful for the time you spent talking to your children, walking with them, telling and showing them that whatever they do or achieve, you will still love and appreciate them for themselves. Spend time with them and consider what makes you too busy sometimes, as they may soon be out of reach. We look back and thank God for the heartache because it has taught us all endurance and patience and brought something to our family life which has drawn us together rather than driven us apart.

I wanted to show you the success we have experienced in Paul's education to encourage you to bring the best out of your child. Right from Playgroup, up through school, college, and now to Polytechnic, Paul has been the same person, he has experienced heartache and pain, joy and sorrow, laughter and tears, negative and positive input into his life and numerous other things that we all experience. It hasn't been as easy for him as some other teenagers, even his brother and sister, Barry and Ruth, but through it he has learnt that we are for him and God is for him. He knows that whatever situation he is in, bottom of the class or top of the class – we love him, he is secure in this.

Let me encourage you to allow your children to develop at their own rate, don't push them into something that you wish for, take time to hear what they say. Don't ignore it because it isn't quite what you would have liked; they are individuals, people in their own right, not just an extension of mum and dad! Love them, tell them you do, and you will build into them security so that they will want to succeed and will want to do their best. But remember, their best may be the bottom of the group and not the top! Be encouraged by Paul's progress but remember, it didn't just happen, it took hours, days, weeks, terms and years of assessing attitudes and motives, of being prepared to be exposed, and giving time and energy even when we felt we had none left. We delight in the amazing way that God stepped into this situation but prior to this we all had to work very hard and Paul still does. It has been worth it all.

During the summer holidays of 1985, Paul worked on a project with another young man in designing a word processor which will be used on computer courses in many colleges. He looked at problems and found a way through. He faced frustration and, against all odds, he would find a way through. His determination and motivation is such.

In October 1985 Andy and I drove back from Wolverhampton with hearts full of joy and gladness, as we had just taken Paul up to the Polytechnic to study for a B.Sc. (Hons.) degree course in computer science. We miss him very much now he is away from home studying. I miss him especially when the computer goes wrong!

The week before Paul went off to Polytechnic, a strange thing happened. He suddenly became ill and was quite delirious with a high temperature. He was like this for twenty four hours. It was very similar to the way he had been after God touched him at the Dales. He lay in bed not wanting to move. We were a little worried as two days later he was due to start college. But then God spoke into my mind. He said, 'I am completing the healing I commenced. Paul is whole.' Thank you, Father, for your love!

14

Interwoven Family Relationships

LOOK BEHIND CLOSED DOORS at family life and what do you see? . . . TV, children, noise, nappies, fighting, arguments, tears, laughter, fun, tiredness, dad reading his newspaper? There are hundreds of things that spring to our minds at the words 'family life'. It may hold for you a lovely memory of serenity, peace, being accepted, oneness, wholeness. But it may hold many heartaches – the place of not being accepted, never being able to live up to what is expected of you, never being right, not dressing correctly or not matching up to your parent's standards at school. You remember the sadness of parents ignoring each other, fighting, not enough money. Maybe a lot of money and possessions, but no one to hug you, no one with time to walk with you, to look at the flowers, birds, trains. The weariness you felt from mum who was always working and had very little time. Of course 'it was all for your good.' But there was no fun, no romance, no sparkle, only pretence when people visited the home.

What is it all about? . . . the joy of love, wanting to be near each other, lingering and dreaming of the future together. Dreams . . . Are they only dreams? This is what your parents thought, but look how it turned out. They, as you, experienced the feeling of life within the womb. What a wonder! What a responsibility! What a joy! But this little bundle has brought so much on the family. So often children are blamed for things that go wrong, lack of time, money, energy. The very life you thought would bring you together is destroying you. Do you know this feeling? Does it have to be this way? You tell yourself you must cope, but can you?

What is the answer? . . . Does it have to be the same for you and your children? . . . It is natural to act toward our children as our parents acted toward us, or treat our husband or wife as our parents treated each other. We feel we are caught up in something over which we have no control. 'Life will go on,' we say, but I have an answer for you. There is a better way, a way of love and peace. This does not mean that you will be immune from problems or difficulties, no . . . but you will have a friend to help you. Somebody who really loves you. This is Jesus. He is alive. He can meet your need, He can bring a new love to you for your wife, your husband, your children, your parents. He wants to bring love and security to your home. He is very powerful but will not force Himself on you, He waits to be invited in.

We, the Croall family, invite you into our home, we want to share with you a little part of our family life. We are a normal family, we have faced and do face joy, sorrow, heartache and pain. We are not immune from these things but we can look at them confidently knowing that God, through His Holy Spirit, is living through us. We are not 'religious', we have great fun, we love parties, we celebrate and dance, we laugh and cry, we work, we pay a mortgage, we have stress and sickness. The kids have their friends around, the music is loud, the dog needs walking, the garden needs tending, homework has to be done. The phone never ceases ringing, the doorbell goes often, the car breaks down, the bikes get punctures. Andy works full time in the Social Services and it is a very demanding job. I teach one evening a week at college and do some secretarial work with 'Satellite Management International' (Technical Co-ordinators for the Satellite/ Video Teleconferencing for the Billy Graham Organisation), and besides this I run a home and counsel quite a lot. We experience the same problems and frustrations that you do, yet very often people from varied walks of life comment on our family relationships. Comments are made like: 'I saw you two walking hand in hand. You looked like two young things in love,' or, 'Your children are so confident and yet respectful', or 'They are so well disciplined.' May I just say that although our children are well disciplined we have never used physical force on them. We have found that, in our experience, if you practise violence on a child, they in turn will do the same. They will feel that the one with the most strength wins. We take time to reason, explain, guide and communicate. Also we mean what we say and say what we mean.

Somebody said to me the other day: 'How do you get your teenagers to do things for you? They seem to listen and respond to what you say.' This is true, they do. It has taken a lot of time and input into their lives to come to this point, but it is beautiful and we are glad we have taken the time. Andy and I have been able to work out our marriage relationship together and then have been able to feed love into the kids. We look at Paul, Barry and Ruth and we realise that God has so carefully placed them in our bands. We treat them as individuals and not just part of ourselves. They have been lent to us for a few short years so that we can help them mature and grow. It is our responsibility to encourage them, discipline them, clothe them, and develop their whole person, body, mind, spirit and emotions.

With Paul's handicap over the years we have been aware of the extra stress on Barry and Ruth. We have tried to keep it an open subject and communicate on the difficulties that may arise. They have been tremendous kids. They have been hurt when thoughtless youngsters have said things about Paul. Time was always short but we realised the benefit of both Andy and me spending time alone with each child individually. I had plenty of opportunities but Andy's diary was always so full he had to book time to spend with the kids.

Last year he and Barry went off to France for a long weekend. They chatted about lots of things, especially motor bikes! We felt it was a critical time in Barry's teenage life. No, he wasn't having any big problems but we wanted to avoid them. Both Andy and Barry just needed time to drive, play, talk, joke and be together. Sometimes Andy and Ruth go up to the Midlands to visit Paul for the weekend. Ruth, in her teens, loves Andy and he loves her. They just need time to talk and listen to each other. No, I don't feel left out or jealous. I feel it is such an investment in the lives of our teenagers to spend time on their own with their dad. He's such a busy person but he fully understands and appreciates the difficulties that emotionally deprived children face. It is so necessary just to be friends with your children.

One thing Andy misses, now Paul has gone off to college, is walking and talking together while exercising Digby, our Bearded Collie dog. They did this nearly every night before bed. They would look at the stars, watch the ducks asleep on the river bank and chat about college, work, computers, church, family, parachuting and anything that was appropriate that day. These times are so precious, grasp them while you have the opportunity and avoid being so busy in other people's lives and ignoring the precious ones that God has placed in your hands.

We have found as a family that we cannot be insular. We have to relate to the wider community. Our lives are spent constantly rubbing shoulders with other people and we enjoy this. Whether it is at work, school, shopping, the theatre, launderette, church, or simply walking the dog. We love people, all kinds of people.

When we moved to our new home, we decided to invite about forty households from our estate to a Sunday afternoon tea. We had a tortoise when we arrived, called Dilla, which was similar to our pony and kept escaping! People brought her back from far and near. We had a little notice which we displayed on our gate-post when she had gone on safari. Unfortunately, the last time she never came back. She was well known on the estate within three months of our arriving here. On our 'Would like to meet the neighbours' invitation we had a large picture of a tortoise with the writing inside it. It was very effective and nearly all the families we invited arrived, so that both our house and garden were packed. The local publican from The Bell came with a great big bottle of wine. Parents, children, single people, one parent families, teenagers and senior citizens all came. It was lovely. On our front lawn we had made a great big playpen with lots of toys in it for the toddlers. It looked so exciting that we had a job keeping some adults out! We all thoroughly enjoyed the afternoon.

We all have a choice. We can enjoy our involvement with other people or we can cut ourselves off and become isolated. Like the old song says, 'I am a rock, I am an island.' As we rub shoulders with other people, we can be like an island, lonely and bitter. Or we can come into contact with others and be flexible and full of life. As I said, we have found as a family that we cannot be insular. We have to relate to the wider community so we are all touched and influenced by our peers.

Earlier in 1985 Wynne Samuel, one of our house-group leaders and the Wycombe Youth Office, and I were running a six week course on Family Relationships. It was particularly aimed at parents with teenagers. One evening, when I was leading the group, the theme was 'Communication'. We looked at how we interact and communicate with our teenagers and how they have to communicate and interact with us and the other important people in their lives. We communicate even if we don't say a lot. We partake in verbal and non-verbal communication. Although I was teaching these people, the awareness of the pressures my own teenagers face dawned on me. The visual aid I used was like this:

The teenager is in the middle of this complex circle. Surrounded by family, peers, friends, and all the other outside influences. Each teenager has to deal with a very complex situation to bring all these pressures into some kind of alignment. Be gentle with them. We may feel that because they are our children they must always please us. Look at all the other pressures on their life. They have to relate to their peer group, which is sure to bring conflict into their lives. They want to be accepted at school and don't want to be different. It isn't surprising that sometimes the parent has to be sensitive enough to step into the background to allow the child to relate on these different levels.

Ruth, our teenage daughter, loves us and we love her. Sometimes she would prefer us to remain in the other room while she talks to somebody. We recognise that we are all individuals and respect her need for privacy sometimes, as she respects ours. It is so easy to discourage your offspring from relating to others as they would wish. It may seem cheeky or inappropriate. The attitude 'children should be seen and not heard' is often carried in our subconscious, so we put our children off certain areas. Ask yourself, when do children become adults? It doesn't just happen in one day. No, you have to allow them to speak, to communicate, to express what their heart is saying.

I have a friend whose husband died quite quickly when only fifty-one years old. Kees was a big, healthy man, over six feet tall and a typical business man. But he developed a tumour on his liver and died of cancer. For many years his wife, Marcia, had prayed for him to know Jesus in a real and personal way. Andy used to talk to him and challenge him about his life. Eventually, and much to our surprise and that of Marcia, he said he would like to be baptised, that is to actually be immersed in water.

I have never forgotten that night. This big man got up in front of his wife, his children and the church of about two hundred people, and spoke about his life. It was December 1983 and he appeared physically strong and healthy. As he got up he began to cry. He had always appeared so confident but as he spoke the whole atmosphere was charged with the power of the Holy Spirit. He said:

'As I look around many of you will wonder why on earth I am here. You'll be surprised to see me here at all. It has taken a long time for me to reach this point and I want to tell you why. It goes back to my own family upbringing as a child.' At this point Kees convulsed with sobs. 'I don't want to be disrespectful. As a child Christianity was never discussed. My parents were Christians in their hearts but it was a Christianity that was only surface deep. We had no religious books and religion was a banned topic.' His words were haltering as he continued to speak. 'When I was thirteen years old I was sent to a boarding school which was run by priests. There I think I got the sort of background which I would classify as a first-class education as to why one should not accept Christianity.

'These people were bigotted, intolerant and totally un-Christian in their attitude to the four hundred boys in their school, and I was one who did not come from their denomination. That has left me pretty scarred and very battered. I may look solid on the outside but I'm not inside, with that sort of background. When I was fourteen years old, one of the priests who was a real Christian spent time with me. We had loads of discussions and that's when I first heard of Christianity and how it was supposed to be.' His sobs overtook him. 'And that good man was struck down by lightning and I never saw him again. The next time I made an attempt to get towards Christianity was when I met Marcia, both before we got married and for about one year after. But it just didn't work. I couldn't get myself through the barriers. I have, in fact, tried on a few occasions since and failed every time. I've hidden my hurt. I've hidden how hard I've tried. I've joked about it. I've pretended I'm not really interested but it hasn't been true. I've done that for twenty five years of our married life and it hurts. Marcia has had faith all along. She never wavered, and I feel it's a disgrace really that I couldn't get there sooner. This last attempt started around the middle of 1980. I've tried different tactics. I've tried reading less and listening more. Looking at people and observing how they behave and somehow or other it seems to have come together a bit better.

'I chose in 1981 to do some work with the Salvation Army and their example has been a leading light to me. Then a group of people in St. Thomas's, Holtspur, prayed for me. They prayed hard. They tried. I know they tried. The people here have prayed for me.

'Now I am coming to what was a big change and tremendous encouragement. My son, Nicholas, was baptised in June 1981 and I saw he changed after he got baptised. The realisation suddenly dawned on me that I could be accepted as I was, faults and all. The

Spirit would thereafter help me to change in the way that was necessary. I have that feeling that God has said it's time I came out of the wilderness. So I stand here tonight saying that I am luckier than Moses. He had forty years in the wilderness and he knew there was a Promised Land, but he only saw it. I've had thirty five years in the wilderness and I know that I am going to get to the Promised Land. I'm luckier than he was and I say thank you, Jesus!'

The congregation exploded into clapping and shouting. It was a powerful experience. The leader of the worship continued: 'We're on holy ground.' He then prayed for all the parents that we would not give scars to our children. God can heal them and is doing so, but it is better if we can so love and communicate with our children to avoid these hurts and pains.

In September 1984, Kees began to feel exhausted. He had always been so healthy and didn't really want to see the doctor as he was very busy. Eventually he went and had various tests. By the end of January 1985 it was discovered he had cancer in the liver and was very, very ill and likely to die. He was still working. One day he left the office and visited the cemetery. He commented to Marcia that most people buried there were either very old or very young. There were not many of his age group. As he walked and thought, he rededicated himself to God. He was ready to go. He had sorted out the most important things of life and death. He was at peace about death, although sad for his family. He knew he was going to be with God, yet as a church, it hurt so much to see this man dying. We wanted God to heal him physically. We knew God could but we also knew Kees was ready to go. Everybody was praying for him and he was a well-known and loved character in the town. We spent days seeking God, asking, praying, fasting. Our children were aware of our sadness.

It was getting very near the end for Kees, and Andy and I had planned to visit him one Thursday evening.

He told us how people wanted him healed but he wanted to go. When Ruth realised we were visiting, she asked if we could deliver something for her. It was addressed to 'Marcia and Kees Spoels' and was a poem she had written with a covering note. It would have been very easy for Andy and me to discourage her involvement at this awful time but we knew that God was working in her, and speaking through her, just as he was through us. So we said we would gladly act as postmen. The note read: 'Sorry this is all I've contributed to the "Cheer the Spoels up" campaign but mum and dad say I'm too young to fast and I'm usually asleep during the prayer meetings. So I've no idea what's going on. I only know that God loves us all. I love you and whatever happens it sure is gonna be good! (Romans 8 v 28). LUV Ruf x (Ruth Croall, Community Church, Holtspur).'

This is what she wrote:

To Marcia and Kees.

I overheard some converse,
I listened,
Churned inside
The talk of death
Of morbid things
Of people who had died.
They did not know I knew you,
They didn't
Really care,
They did not believe in miracles
We surely
Had them there.
They said "Maybe a few more months"
(I'm sorry
To speak my friend
On this talk of death and life
Of coming
to the end):

But what is the end?
But a beginning
Of God's joy released to the free
And before the end
The beginnings begun
Cos' Jesus died for you and me
To give us life
To "live it up"
"Up" to the holy throne,
We're all alive
We'll never die
We're living to the bone!
Well, back to the conversation
They had
When I was there
I felt I had a point of view
That God would
Have me share.
I spoke out loud as I felt right
"Kees is going
To live."
"Yes my dear," the woman said
"But in
Another world.
When you're as old as I am
You will not trust your eyes
You'll have enough wisdom
To realise they are lies.
What people have told you
Of miracles and good
You should disregard them
I tell you you should.
You'll understand my dear
When poor Kees dies."
Can I tell you, Marcia,
I hope I never grow that wise!!!
I told her of the prophecies,
But she only laughed at me
"Jesus died when he was man,"

she said, "and so should we."
But Marcia, cheer yourself
For something more was said
A little voice from the back of the room
Squeaked "Jesus rose from the dead."
For what is the end
But a beginning
Of God's joy released to the free,
And before the end
The beginning begun
Cos' Jesus died for you and me
To give us life
To "Live it up"
Right up to Jesu's throne,
We're all alive
We'll never die
We're all on our way home!

Marcia explained to me how at the very deepest time of sorrow children communicated to them. Ruth's poem had been able to verbalise what adults find hard to say. It was just what Marcia and Kees needed during that last week of his life.

The day after Kees died, the house was busy, the family shocked and sorrowing. Some people were disillusioned that God hadn't physically healed Kees. Marcia was relieved that he wasn't suffering anymore. She knew his spirit had gone to be with God. She said, 'Amidst all this sorrow and busyness, there was a knock on the door. Standing there was a little girl called Rachel. She handed me a little bunch of flowers she had picked. A note was pinned to it which read: 'To Mrs. Spoel. I would like you to have this bunch of flowers because Mr. Spoel was a great friend of mine. Love Rachel!'

Marcia was so touched and helped by the children. They are so sensitive and honest. We sometimes are so sophisticated that we miss out on touching people by our lives in case 'we are intruding!' Try to allow your little ones to communicate to the wider community. Don't constantly hold them back because of your own hang-ups.

In relating to the wider community, we sometimes wish it could be in different circumstances. I found this true recently as I was lying on the physiotherapist's couch getting my shoulder treated. It has been a delight to meet Sally Williams. She is a lovely person and very determined to get people well! In a way, I would prefer to have met her in different circumstances, rather than suffering excruciating pain from a shoulder that refuses to move. This problem has been frustrating me now on and off for over three years. It limits me from doing the things I want to, and the things I need to. It has kept me dependent on my family and friends. I must say, I am quite happy for somebody else to do the ironing and vacuuming, but it is very frustrating. Even to fasten my apron I have to ask for help. This situation has involved me in the wider community of the hospital, doctor, nurses. When I visited the consultant and was sitting in the Waiting Room, I looked around the people. It's very interesting, 'human watching'! Some looked as if they didn't have any hope, joy or future. I communicated with some through my eyes. An old lady was so pleased that I had actually smiled at her. The nurse calling the names looked tired. I commented 'You look as if you have been working hard,' and she responded immediately. She somehow felt like a person again. I guess she had been taking names for this busy clinic all afternoon with nobody acknowledging her as a person. We can be very lonely people in a busy, well-populated area.

During Paul's difficulties we were constantly needing to call on people in the community to help us. For many years we used 'Calibre', the tape library for the blind and Dyslexic. This was an invaluable help to Paul when he couldn't read the books he was capable of understanding. On occasions the books he wanted were not on tape. At these times we called on two friends of ours, Mo and Kate, who would spend hours reading books on to a tape for Paul so that he could listen to them. People would type for him. It was amazing how many people wanted to help when they realised the problem.

Another involvement in our lives is through Andy's work. Some of it is very pleasurable and delightful, but some of it is hearbreaking. Recently a little four year old girl had been put in a room and starved to death when in the home of her parents. The Social Services had responded when notified, but it was too late, the little girl was dead. A case like this is so traumatic, so devastating to realise that helpless children get harmed and killed. Andy has to relate on a professional basis to his managers and social workers. Often they are blamed if a child dies; he has to guard against such occurrences, but also encourage his staff in helping these families whose children are so much at risk.

Then we relate to a group of people called the 'Church'. Not the building but the people. Interestingly enough, as a church, we do not have a building. We meet on Sundays in the local Youth Centre, and during the week in homes. We find that in relating to each other, not just on a Sunday but at all times, we are released and fulfilled. We can call on each other to help sort out any family difficulties or marriage problems, and can help to meet each other's needs, financial as well as spiritual and practical.

We have in our church a most beautiful girl. When she smiles, she is so pretty. She has allowed God to touch many intimate areas of her life; things that have hurt her and caused her to become a very angry, bitter young lady. When I first met her, my description of her would have been 'A pot boiling'. She was very angry, she looked it and everyone around felt it. I am not saying she shouldn't have been angry, she had things to be angry about. Life had dealt some hard blows. The problem was that her bitterness and anger were eating her away.

During the sermon one Sunday evening I said, 'Lord, if you want to reveal anything to me, I'm available to be used.' He did. Not what I expected. God gave me a picture of a little baby only just born with the cord only just cut. It was left without human contact and was so angry with the cold world it was in. At the end of the meeting, this young lady came to me, very desperate and said, 'I really need you.' I had put this vision temporarily out of my mind. I thought it was probably for one of the young mums who had just given birth. So I counselled this girl for about twenty minutes. Suddenly I realised the vision was for her. I explained it to her and on that row in the middle of the church building God took her in her emotions and spirit right back to the day of her birth. He held her and assured her that He was never going to let her go. Later we discovered that, at the time of her birth, her mother had been quite ill and totally exhausted. It wasn't her wish not to cuddle this little one but circumstances made it impossible. Her mother really loved her.

This feeling of not being loved was reinforced later when she went to boarding school. Her parents went abroad for a number of years. So this child had reason to be angry but it was destroying her adult life. To see what God has done and is doing is a real pleasure.

It was through this lassie that God confirmed to me that I should write this book. I hadn't shared my thoughts about a book with anyone apart from Andy, but this lovely girl approached me one morning and said 'I was awake last night. As clear as anything God said to me, "Tell Dot Croall to write a book about all the things that I have done." ' My, coming from this lassie that was something! I thanked her for being faithful even when it seemed a strange thing to say.

As we look at our family we see a beautiful family placed in the Body of Christ. We are accepted, faults and all, by our brothers and sisters. I believe that Paul's confidence has grown not just because we took time to help and encourage him, but having a group of people who love him and want the very best for him. This confidence is shown again in Barry and Ruth. They are totally loved and accepted even if they do something wrong.

Through this real life story I want you to endeavour to love your children and to express it. They are going to get some hard knocks in the world, they need to know that you are on their side and not always against them. Work at bringing the best out of them. They have always got something you can praise them about. God has given them to you for a very short time, don't hold them too tightly but develop them into their own person. That is how they will be happiest!

Epilogue

SEEING STRAIGHT has taken just over a year in writing but eighteen years of life's experiences to be ripe enough to share with other families. The effect on each one of the family members of the book being written has been different and varied from the absorption of Dot in producing the manuscript to the delight of Ruth in learning new facts about the family history, but throughout the various memories recalled by incidents identified in the book has kept fresh the reality and enormity of what has happened. The heart of the book has been about an average family facing difficulties which are not too uncommon and finding help and strength in a number of ways open to all.

I believe that many of the experiences in the book will not be new to many parents except the focus on a community of people bearing one another's burdens. The isolation or the retreat of the father or mother which so often occurs on discovering the child has a handicap can lead to a series of actions and attitudes which go on to affect the whole family. So too can the focus on one child to the neglect of another, or the loading of a burden on to an older child. The bad news is that having done what we think is right we later realise that we may have caused damage. The good news is that it is never too late to repair damage! Memories can be healed and the parents find understanding from each other again and reunite the family.

Dot and I have found the sharing of our experiences has enabled others to tackle issues in their own lives and families. During the drafting of the manuscript and the research and discussion with a variety of professional contacts I have become aware of how many of them have similar heartaches and needs. Dot and I have shared our experience in the hope that you will be encouraged by it.

Andy Croall